To Grandma's House, We...Stay

To Grandma's House, We...Stay

When You Have to Stop Spoiling Your Grandchildren
and Start Raising Them

Sally Houtman, M.S.

Studio 4 Productions
Northridge, CA

To Grandma's House, We...Stay

When You Have to Stop Spoiling Your Grandchildren and Start Raising Them

Copyright 1999 by Studio 4 Productions
Published by Studio 4 Productions
Post Office Box 280400
Northridge, CA 91328-0400

Library of Congress Catalog Card Number: 98-61478

ISBN: 1-882349-05-9

Editor: Bob Rowland

Book Design: Carey Christensen

Cover Design: Bob Aulicino

To Dorothy Stock and to the loving memory of
Ralph Stock, Sr.,
"Mom" and "Pop"—
the grandparents to whom I owe so very much,
and to grandparents everywhere,
whose loving sacrifice becomes our grateful legacy.

Table of Contents

When Spring and Summer come then pass,
And Autumn's calm bids peace at last,
What fateful tug at nature's string
Has turned the Autumn back to Spring?

The sleeping rose when stirred must rise,
Its bloom may tire but never dies,
A castaway adrift no more
Has washed upon love's waiting shore.

The Author

1

Becoming a Parent–Again

Taking on the responsibility of raising your grandchildren is an enormous commitment. Just being a parent in the first place requires commitments that go far beyond anyone's expectations. Having already been through it once, no one knows better than a parent the time, the patience, the sacrifices, the struggles, and the worries that go along with this role. Yet no one knows better than a parent the joys, the rewards, the pride, and the satisfaction this role can also bring.

But there is no denying that things are very different the second time around. You're older and in a very different place in your life. Yes, along with age come knowledge and experience, some of which you may wish you had the first time; however, the energy, stamina, patience, and enthusiasm you once had in great abundance may now be in short supply.

Chances are, when you first became a parent, you had more time (at least nine months' worth) to plan, prepare, and adjust both emotionally and financially to the upcoming changes. If your experience is like that of most, you didn't get the preparation time as a grandparent to make the lifestyle adjustments needed in order to accommodate becoming a parent the second time. Children come to parents with advance notice. Grandchildren, on the other hand, often come to their grandparents with little or no warning. What begins as a temporary stay often turns into a permanent arrangement. Whatever the circumstances, the grandparents are seldom prepared.

It's also likely that when you became a grandparent, the joy of the occasion hadn't yet been clouded by the realization that you would someday be responsible for the care of your grandchildren. After all, wasn't it just *supposed* to be your privilege as a grandparent to be a background player in the lives of your grandchildren?

In a perfect world, grandparents certainly deserve the luxury of enjoying their brief and periodic visits with their grandchildren. And they have clearly earned the right during those visits to indulge in the time-honored tradition of spoiling their grandchildren absolutely rotten.

If things are as they *should* be, the role of grandparent carries with it certain privileges. It seems not just the right but nearly the responsibility of a grandparent to lovingly undermine parental authority by breaking every rule the parent has worked so hard to enforce. Grandparents are *supposed* to give their grandchildren goodies they're not allowed to have. Grandparents are *supposed* to allow their grandchildren pleasures and privileges that are otherwise forbidden. It's *supposed* to be part of the special bond between grandparent and grandchild for them to cherish these secret pleasures and to remain blissfully silent about them.

But perhaps the most eagerly awaited privilege a grandparent has comes when the time arrives for changing, scolding, cleaning up after, or disciplining children. It's that treasured time when the grandparent hands the children back to their weary parents for maintenance. Grandparents deserve to enjoy all of the perks with none of the mess.

That's simply the way it's *supposed* to be, right? That is, at least when things are as they should be.

It's the natural order of things for parents to encourage their children to become independent, self-sufficient individuals. It's then the parents' right to sit comfortably in the background, satisfied that their job has been done to the best of their ability. In adulthood, the path each child now chooses is of his or her own making. This frees the parent to at last step back and serve more as an advisor, a support system, an equal, and a friend. As the natural order progresses, age and maturity allow the now "adult child" to begin giving back to the parent. Over the course of their lives, the roles of parent and child will gradually shift and eventually reverse.

And after all, shouldn't age have its privileges? With their children grown and on their own, parents have the right at long last to reclaim their lives as their own. Once the children are grown, there's time for parents to get to know one another again. It can be an understandably awkward time when they have the chance to reach back into their faded memories to recall that long-forgotten time when they were once a couple...before they became a family.

Without the common distraction of children between them, parents now have an opportunity to become reacquainted. For couples, it's a time for building and rebuilding, a time for re-evaluating the direction their lives have taken. It's also a time for reflecting and paving the road to their futures—whether it be together or separately.

For single parents, this time can be a long-awaited break from bearing the weight of being both father and mother. For many, it's the first time they've had a chance to get to know themselves as individuals apart from being parents. Whatever the case, this should be a time for parents to take a deep breath of long-anticipated freedom. It's their chance to discover new and creative uses for the empty rooms in the house, and it's time for them to get reacquainted with the long-forgotten indulgence of having money to spend on themselves. Who knows...they might even make a reality out of that life-long dream vacation on their own, without the kids. Sounds perfect, doesn't it?

But our world is less than perfect, and our circumstances are seldom ideal. We know all too well that the way we think things *ought* to be seems closer to fantasy than reality, so it's important that we take care to remain fair and realistic. It seems that our fantasy ideas of the way things are supposed to be would provide a better plot for a TV movie than a realistic standard against which to measure our own experience.

The truth is, those fictional families many of us still use to judge how things should be, are becoming extinct. The traditional family system as it once was (and as many of us think it still should be) is slowly disappearing, perhaps another tragic casualty of our changing times. As the pressures and problems of today's life become more abundant, more destructive, and more complex, the family system as we know it has had to bend in response. More and more, the nuclear family of the past seems to have become the rare exception to a long-forgotten rule.

So what happened to the family of the past? The reasons for the changing face of our families are as complex as the problems they create. Some hold society responsible for the breaking apart of the family unit. They blame unemployment, low wages, and the lack of educational opportunities. After all, how can we be expected to succeed and to make a better life for our children when we're forced to do so much more with so much less?

Others blame drugs, crime, and the lure of easy money for creating an environment where mere survival is the name of the game. When it's every man for himself, rusty family virtues such as cooperation, consideration, and "helping our fellow man" can prove to be not only unrealistic, but in some cases even deadly. Whatever the case, the term *family* has become more synonymous with increasing demands on decreasing resources than with a unit to which we're forever bound by unwavering loyalty.

To top it off, there are those among us who cite all of the above as proof that our society is on a collision course with disaster, and that it's taking our families with it!

Regardless of the reason, we can't afford to waste precious energy wondering why we're in the position we're in or trying to figure out how we got here. When you're caught in a trap, it doesn't matter how you fell into it. Once you're there, it's important to focus on putting together a plan of escape. If we as families have fallen victim to society's ills, cursing society for our plight may make us feel a bit better, but it won't help us get by. The captain of a sinking ship will surely drown if his attention is devoted entirely to measuring the size of the hole in his vessel and determining the exact cause of the leak. And his fate would be equally grim if his final energies were spent cursing the ship for failing him. At such desperate moments, knowing *why* the ship is sinking won't keep it from going down. The fact is, families are changing. We can either bail with all our might or look for a lifeboat.

We certainly can't deny that the growing phenomenon of grandparents raising their grandchildren is in many ways a reflection of broader social problems. As violent crime, gangs, drugs, AIDS, divorce, and teen pregnancy rise to epidemic proportions, a generation of children is left in their wake. Determining the breadth and scope of these problems, charting the demographics, and analyzing the general social trends that create such family problems is best left to the experts. For the grandparents and grandchildren who wage daily battle on the front lines, statistics and theories offer little in the way of practical solutions to their day-to-day problems.

You don't have to be a statistician to know that if you've found yourself on the path from parenthood to grandparenthood, only to be routed back to parenthood again, you're not alone. Things are difficult enough when life follows its expected course (the number of books on the general subject of parenting quickly confirms this notion). Your path has been diverted from the expected course, therefore, the difficulties you will encounter will be unique and the problems you'll come across will be unexpected. You now find yourself faced with not only the prospect of being a parent again, but also with the additional task of redefining the whole concept of *family* as you once knew it.

It's a fact that more and more grandparents are raising their grandchildren these days. It's also true that this issue has received relatively little public attention to date. Unless they are directly affected, people aren't likely to give the situation a passing thought. Historically, grandparents have always served as stand-in parents when the need arose. But in the past it seems that this need arose with much less frequency and only under dire circumstances. When it did occur, those affected were commonly the subject of curiosity, raised eyebrows, and hushed speculation in dark corners. The absent or negligent parents were harshly judged while the charitable grandparents received a mixture of admiration and pity. Depending on the specifics of their situation, those grandparents tried to keep their struggles a secret. They felt alone and burdened by both the weight of being responsible for the family's survival and their feelings of shame for being in that position in the first place.

Also in times past, the circumstances that created absentee parents were typically sources of either great disgrace or great compassion. What if the parents were killed in a tragic accident? If this were the case, the orphaned children were pitied and the grieving grandparents consoled. Perhaps the parents had fallen ill or become disabled, in which case similar feelings were brought up in sympathetic onlookers. Events such as these that brought grandparents and grandchildren together were easily excused as random acts of fate or circumstances beyond anyone's control.

In times past as well, those occasions in which parents abandoned or neglected their parental responsibilities seemed comparatively rare. When this did occur, it was too taboo to discuss and excuses were sometimes offered for the parents' behavior. If the truth were told, embarrassment and shame were the end result. The "immoral" father or mother who had so carelessly left the children with the grandparents to run off with another mate was believed to have committed an unspeakable crime. Judgment and suspicion were cast upon any parent who demonstrated such weakness of character.

A similar fate awaited the parents who gave in to the "evils" of alcohol or (God forbid) drugs, which rendered them incapable of managing their parental responsibilities. Society's intolerance for such behavior held parents to a higher standard, but it also often cast an unfortunate shadow on the children that we know as the "sins of the fathers" scenario.

It's a mixed blessing that society has become more tolerant and understanding of such behaviors. The drawback takes the form of our grim realization that the family is no longer a unit, as it once was. Today's families come in all varieties as each family unit adjusts, conforms, and at times collapses under the weight of society's increasing and ever-changing demands. But there is also some sadness for us as we witness the family unit becoming increasingly fragmented. As a result, the families of today are forced to rise to the unique challenge of redefining themselves. As pressures mount and the task of sticking together becomes ever more difficult, it is essential that we who find ourselves thrust together in that essential framework we call a *family* work tirelessly to maintain our cohesiveness in the face of chaos.

In reality, rather than using these pressures to bring us together as families, many of us are allowing them to pull us apart. Only blame and bitterness will thrive in the empty spaces where parents once were. Those children who are left to feel abandoned realize quickly that the relentless pursuit of self-preservation is the only way to make it in this world. Cynical and mistrustful, they learn that if they can't trust others, they have to learn to use them to their advantage. Lacking direction and doubtful that others care, they feel they must take matters into their own hands.

It's an unfortunate reality that many of our children are growing up on their own and are becoming more and more indifferent. Loose or nonexistent ties to a family system in childhood lay the groundwork for adults whose only weapon against helplessness and complete vulnerability is their callous disregard for the feelings of others. Children who feel they cannot trust others to look after their well-being become adults who are incapable of feeling compassion or concern toward the well-being of others.

Rather than cast a judgmental eye on these youths, it's better for us to understand how they came to be so—not only because we're at least partially responsible for creating them, but also because we owe it to them and to ourselves to realize that everyone is worth saving, and that it's never too late to turn things around. Individuals aren't born mistrustful, bitter, or unfeeling; it's experience that makes them that way. Without love, guidance, and acceptance, the emotional blisters of childhood can too easily turn into calluses. This does not at all suggest that the decay of the family is solely responsible for the problems of today's youth, but it is a painful acknowledgment that this is undoubtedly a contributing factor.

Our family is the first and most important unit in which we feel a sense of belonging or a sense of responsibility to others. Our family teaches us that we play a role within a larger social unit. It's a dress rehearsal for the role we'll eventually play in society as a whole. It's likely the only system we'll ever belong to that is capable of giving us the experience of being nurtured, a feeling of safety and security, and a feeling of permanence. Parents are responsible for providing stability for their children, and children will *always* suffer when it's not there. On a larger scale, one could say that a tragic toll is taken on individuals when they are betrayed by the very system that is designed to protect them.

In the face of these realities, it's too easy to develop a defeatist attitude toward the times we live in. It would be easy for us to moan bitterly about the way things are and sing the praises of the "good old days," but that gets us nowhere and only makes us sound like the crabby old cynic we swore we'd never become. Instead, it's better for us to search inside ourselves and try to make some sense out of the confusion. After all, we have just two choices: we can either dwell on the problem, or become part of the solution.

Criticism, like a spectator sport, requires virtually no risk. But if we take the easy route and shout from the sidelines, we miss our chance to play on the winning team. Sure, it's more difficult and riskier for us to accept the fact that times are changing, like it or not, but it's best to get in the game.

Many of us make the sad mistake of believing that if we don't like the rules, we don't have to play the game. But it is this author's belief that it's not important that we like the rules; it's important that we become involved and make the best of the situation. It's important that we keep in mind that our best chance of finding happiness in the face of changing times is to realize that our unhappiness doesn't come so much from change as it does from our resistance to it.

More than likely, we can all recall a time when the nontraditional family was viewed with cautious curiosity. Much to our surprise and perhaps dismay, we may be approaching a point in history where the intact family is viewed with that same curiosity. We have to work harder these days to create a sense of traditional family stability in nontraditional circumstances. If we look hard enough to find something positive about our unfavorable circumstances, we might be able to take comfort in knowing that our changing times are forcing us all to be more flexible in our thinking.

As we begin to accept that things are not as they once were on the home front, we are forced to change our ideas and gain a newfound responsibility to become more open-minded. Let's face it, the traditional family of the past is still the ideal. But if our situation doesn't measure up, should we spend our lives cursing the heavens for shortchanging us? Or shall we bend our rigid definition of *family* so that we can all find a sense of belonging and togetherness, no matter how unconventional our individual circumstance might be? The choice, of course, is always our own.

If there is nothing else positive to say about our changing definition of *family*, perhaps we can be reluctantly grateful that in comparison, the unique problems of any given family seem no more peculiar than those of the next. At the very least, we are spared the harsh moral judgments that were once the order of the day. If we can come to appreciate our own situation as being *unique* instead of *dysfunctional,* we have a much better chance of finding a richness and fulfillment, no matter what our situation might be. We have a lot to gain when we shift our focus away from what we seem to be lacking by someone else's standards and back to that which we already possess.

Regardless of the events that have conspired to thrust grandparent and grandchild together, the aftermath is much the same. No matter whether this happens frequently or seldom, whether it is accepted or stigmatized, the fact remains that a generation is missing in between. Part of the dilemma facing those on either side of this missing generation is the problem of what to do with the empty space. And part of the challenge facing both sides is the daunting task of building a bridge across this chasm.

But long before the bridge construction can or should begin, the first consideration is whether or not you feel up to this undertaking and are ready to face this challenge. Long before the building materials are ordered or the construction crew is brought on site, it will be not only valuable but also vital for you to evaluate your desire and ability to do the job and to do it well. A thorough, honest, and realistic inventory of what you've got to work with will help you to assess the scope of the job and decide if the job is truly for you. The chapters that follow will guide you through the considerations you'll need to face, the skills you'll need to learn, and the obstacles you'll no doubt encounter on your journey from parent to grandparent...and back again.

2

Making the Commitment to Raise a Second Family

By the time you read these words, many of you will already have accepted the challenge of reaching across the generation gap and becoming a parent again. Some of you may yet be struggling, trying to decide whether to do it or not. And the rest of you may be on the verge of the dawning realization that the short-term arrangement you had originally agreed to is looking more permanent than temporary. Regardless, it's still of value for you to take a closer look at your options and your motivations. Doing so, even if after the fact, will make certain that you've fully considered the ramifications such an enormous decision will have on your life and on the lives of the others in your family circle.

Those of you who have already made the choice to become parents again may consider it pointless to look at the motives behind a decision that has already been made. Nonetheless, it is worth the time and consideration in order for you to appreciate the benefits and drawbacks of your choice and to better understand your reasons for making it, even if in retrospect. Being crystal clear about your motives and expectations certainly doesn't change the reality of the situation, but it can give you a greater understanding of the nature of the conflicts, both internal and external, you'll encounter. It will also better prepare you for the broad and unforeseen ways this decision will change your life.

Before we begin, understand that if you're not completely and brutally honest with yourself about what inspired you to step into the lives of your grandchildren, you'll unknowingly be dishonest about the expectations you'll have of yourself and others. We always owe it to ourselves to be completely honest about our goals and expectations in any major choice we make. It's also important for us to have a clear understanding of the fact that, as humans and as rational and thinking beings, we have choices available to us at all times. Even in situations in which we feel we have no options, we are still making choices. When grandparents explain why they took in their grandchildren by saying, *"I had no choice—there was nothing else I could do"*—it may not be entirely true.

A Few Words about Choice

In the real world, there are few times we'll ever find ourselves with no real choices—times when we are truly forced to do something against our will. Whether we accept a course of action or reject it, we are making a choice. Likewise, allowing others to make decisions on our behalf, and allowing them to coerce or manipulate us or place unwanted responsibility on us are choices we make. Each of these requires our participation. It's a common error in our thinking to blame others for forcing us into undesirable situations. If we're willing at all times to accept the part we play in any situation, we'll be better able to avoid the miserable trap of trying to make others responsible for our circumstances and ultimately our destinies.

One of the most common and potentially destructive pitfalls lying in wait for grandparents who are faced with the choice of taking in their grandchildren is their well-intended but nonetheless false belief that they have no choice in the matter. If you are in this situation, it's quite likely that no one openly offered you a choice. But don't forget that once we become adults, no individual has the power to make a decision on our behalf without our consent. It's more likely that we're guilty by omission because our failure to express an opinion can easily be interpreted as consent (as they say, silence can sometimes speak louder than words), and failure to take action is, in itself, a conscious act.

No one will argue how heart-wrenching and painful it is to be placed in the position of determining the fate of a child. It's doubly difficult when the child is one you didn't participate in creating. Whether or not you decide to accept the job of caring for this child, accept responsibility for choosing whatever role you decided to play in his or her life. Even if there seemed to be no reasonable alternative, accept that your decision was a conscious choice on your part. Avoid compounding the burdens you are already carrying by adding to them the feeling that you were backed into a corner with no way out. There are always options, realistic or unrealistic as they may seem at the moment.

Foster homes? Distant relatives? Godparents? Strangers? *"What kind of choices are these?"* many exclaim. Although they may not seem realistic or even appealing alternatives to many, they are options just the same. If you feel you'd rather sleep for eternity on a bed of broken glass than subject your grandchild to the foster care system, you're not alone in this sentiment. If you have opted to raise the child yourself rather than hand over his or her care to the unknown, then take pride in this decision. Don't make the mistake of turning this situation into one more problem you've been left to solve that you didn't cause. Don't sell yourself—or all those hours you spent agonizing over this decision—so short. Accept that you have weighed the options, however briefly, and have in the end deemed them all unsuitable.

Maggie

Maggie, a divorced mother of three grown children, sat in her therapist's office with her head in her hands. Her 30-year-old son, Jack, had really done it this time. "I can't believe he's back in jail," she moaned. "He's only been out a month. I don't understand it. I guess he'll never stop messing with those drugs!"

And then there was Josh, Jack's 18-month-old son. Josh's mother was a longtime heroin addict who'd been in and out of prison herself the past few years. The mother had sent Josh to stay with her older sister temporarily when the new boyfriend she was living with took to beating her. The plan was for Josh to return to his father when he got back on his feet. So much for that plan.

"Of course, she called _me_ last night in a panic the minute she heard that Jack got picked up again," Maggie cried. "She's been anxious to get Josh off her hands, so now she thinks I'm the answer to her prayers."

"So what are you going to do?" the therapist asked.

"What do you mean, what am I going to do?" Maggie snapped indignantly. "Like I really have a choice!"

"Of course, you have a choice," the therapist replied in her best therapeutic tone. "We always have choices."

"Oh, sure, just leave Josh with a woman who doesn't care about him, or drop him off at the nearest foster home," Maggie groaned. "Some choice!"

As the session went on, Maggie began to see that she was feeling pressured into taking care of Josh the same way she'd felt roped into bailing her son out of every jam he'd ever gotten himself into.

"So Josh is just another one of Jack's messes you have to clean up...is that what you're saying?"

Maggie couldn't help but feel offended. "How could you say a thing like that?" she said. "He's my grandson. You don't seem to understand how many times Jack has done this to me. I'm tired of it! Only this time it means I have to put my entire life on hold because of him."

"And you'll never miss an opportunity to remind him of it, will you?"

With gentle prodding, Maggie was able to realize that she had been setting up a disaster plan in her mind. Angry that no one had taken her feelings into consideration but instead had just made the assumption like they always did that she'd take Josh in, she felt she'd been backed into a corner with no way out.

"So you're not sure about taking Josh in?" the therapist asked.

"That's not the point," Maggie said. "Did anyone ever stop to think about what this was going to do to me? I wish someone had asked before just assuming that I could handle taking care of Josh."

"So because no one asked you, you're going to use this to stay angry with Jack and Josh's mother so they'll never forget that they should have checked with you before they got high and made a baby?"

Maggie's longstanding distaste for her son's lifestyle was finally coming to a head. She was creating a scenario in which, because *she'd been pressured into taking care of Josh, she'd use her inconvenience as a weapon to forever hold over her son's head. You see, Maggie had every reason to be angry, but she needed to find some other way of dealing with it than using it to make everyone feel guilty about how their carelessness was affecting her.*

Maggie did take Josh in, and by looking at what part she had played in setting herself up to look like a victim, she was able to take responsibility for him by choice rather than by force. She was able to learn how to keep her anger at her son from clouding her decision to take care of Josh. She also came to the realization that she didn't have to stay upset about having to take Josh in to show her son that she disapproved of his way of life. By putting her anger in its proper place, she took back her power and was able to rise to the occasion of being a stand-in parent for Josh because it was the right thing to do, not because it was expected of her.

Most grandparents will take on the overwhelming chore of raising their grandchildren in the spirit that it's really the only reasonable thing to do from both a practical and a humanitarian standpoint. The majority of grandparents faced with this decision couldn't bear the thought of turning their grandchildren over to the care of strangers or trusting a complex and seemingly insensitive bureaucratic system to make decisions of lasting importance on their grandchildren's behalf. This is precisely the reason why so many grandparents find themselves raising their grandchildren. In most cases, it just makes the most sense.

It seems to be the most decent and benevolent thing for the sake of the children to remain within the family. But this may not be the case for everyone. The truth is, not all children who are in need belong with their grandparents. The most important consideration is that whatever decision is made, it is ultimately made in the best interest of the *child*. If the grandparents are not in a position, whether financially, emotionally, physically, or otherwise, to manage this responsibility, it may well be in the best interest of the child to entrust the job to someone more able.

Is It Love, or Just Obligation?

The point being made here is that, whatever the decision, it must be realistic and stem from love rather than obligation. Be careful not to get lured into that deceptive trap we call *obligation*. Although a strong sense of family obligation is not in itself a bad thing, it can complicate matters by once again leading us to believe that we've been stripped of our choices. *"But what else could I do?"* you may cry. Nothing, perhaps. But whatever we do for another person, whether it be family or friend, it is best done because we *can*, or because it's the right thing, not because we feel we *must*. The consequence of doing things purely out of obligation is that it will cause us to feel angry and resentful in the long run. Many grandparents who feel obligated to take in their grandchildren spend a lot of time secretly feeling angry about having to do it, which in turn causes them to spend even more time denying they're angry. After all, if they're just doing what's in the best interest of the family, they've got no reason to feel angry, right?

Wrong. The anger comes less from the responsibility they've taken on than from their failure to recognize their part as a willing participant in the process. In many respects, the situations we find ourselves in are less significant than how we react to finding ourselves in them. We're bound to feel angry when we feel something (even the care of a child) has been thrust on us against our will. Even when the thing we're asked to do is something we truly wouldn't mind doing, we're still angry because we feel *obligated* to do it. The fact of the mater is that, in reality, we don't ever have to feel this way if we change our point of view.

It becomes critical for us to understand that our anger in these situations is our own creation. Instead of concentrating on what we have to do, we get caught up in resenting the fact that we're stuck doing something we wouldn't otherwise have chosen to do. If this is the case, we've forgotten one basic principle: we don't always get to choose the situations with which life confronts us, but that doesn't mean we don't have a choice in how we handle them. Let's face it, we all want to feel in control. We all want to feel that somehow the things we do are of our own design and not just things we're expected to do. But doing what is expected of us doesn't mean we've lost control; it just means we've recognized that we can't control what happens to us—we can only control what we decide to do about it. Life becomes easier when we rise to its challenges and stop blaming others for putting obstacles in our path.

Here is an example of how obligation can lead to anger:

Martha

Martha and her 19-year-old daughter, Rebecca, decided that Rebecca would remain at home after her son was born. Martha felt it was the only reasonable thing for them all, since she would be available to watch the baby while Rebecca concentrated on finishing her education.

Every other evening and most weekends, Martha did as she had agreed and watched her grandson while Rebecca was at class. In fulfilling her obligation to Rebecca, Martha began to neglect her own social life. Her justification was that this is what any loving grandmother would do under the circumstances.

Despite Rebecca's offers to pay for a baby-sitter on occasion or to leave the baby with her older sister to give Martha a break, Martha insisted that she was fine with the arrangement. After all, Rebecca's sister had enough to deal with, and they could put the money that would have gone to a sitter to better use.

As time went on, however, Martha began to feel resentful at having given up her social life. In essence, she began to resent her own generosity. Confused by these feelings, she brushed them off, convinced that no loving grandmother could possibly feel resentful at caring for the grandson she adored so much.

But the more she watched her daughter go off to school, the more she felt taken advantage of. After all, she wasn't the one who had messed up her life by getting pregnant, but she did seem to be the one now suffering because of it.

Her guilt over having such strong resentment caused her to bottle it up. She even started to overcompensate by offering to do more for Rebecca. It seemed like Martha was trying to convince herself that she wasn't really feeling so used, after all.

To ease her guilt, she boasted about how proud she was to see her daughter being so responsible and how happy she was to be able to help.

So you can understand Rebecca's shock the night her standard request for her mother to watch the baby while she had dinner with her classmate was answered with, "Oh, of course I will. I have nothing better to do, you know. I guess any hopes I had of having a life of my own are gone, so one of us might as well have some fun!"

Where on earth did that come from?

Martha had made the tragic mistake of forgetting that she was a willing participant who made a conscious choice to step up to bat for Rebecca. She had led herself to believe that it was her duty, her responsibility, to watch her grandson and that no self-respecting grandmother would do otherwise. Feeling thus obligated, she took on the additional burden of believing that her daughter's education and ability to rise above having had a baby at such a young age was now riding on her as well. And if she failed to live up to her obligation, *she* would be responsible for her daughter's failure to succeed.

The problem with this picture is not that she made herself available to watch her grandson but that she forgot that she *wanted* to do it and began feeling that she *had* to. It was her faulty logic that set her up to feel she'd have failed had she considered other options. Her feeling of *obligation* led her to place unrealistic expectations on herself and her daughter and ultimately opened the door for her resentment.

It may very well have been that it was in everyone's best interest for Martha to watch the baby, but thinking that it was her *obligation* left her feeling unappreciated and taken for granted. Because she was doing something for someone she loved, she felt guilty about her anger and tried to cover it up; but it didn't go away. Instead, it began to appear in the form of sarcastic and biting remarks. Martha's load would have been substantially lightened had she forgiven her daughter for becoming pregnant, forgiven herself for being understandably angry about it, and put that energy to use in making a real difference in her grandson's life.

These characteristics of anger and obligation are offered as examples here in an effort to ease the heavy load shouldered by grandparents who have already taken on enough. By having a thorough understanding of why you feel the way you do and particularly that what you feel is perfectly normal, you won't be adding to the pressure you already feel by passing unfair judgment on yourself.

You can't expect that you'll never feel angry or resentful. Anger, obligation, sadness, regret, and guilt are all a part of the package you fall heir to when you become a parent to your grandchildren. We gain the greatest control over our lives when we understand our feelings and vulnerabilities, take responsibility for them, and stop pretending they don't exist. It's high time to throw away the faulty notion that you're not allowed to be fed up with someone you love. When you deny that they've hurt you, disappointed you, or let you down, you're playing a game of make-believe with the ones you love. We should show one another more respect than this. Our fears, hurts, and resentments gain power only if we deny they exist and then feel trapped when we pretend that others haven't hurt us in some small way. You may already feel trapped by your circumstances; don't allow yourself to be held hostage by your feelings as well.

Beware of Blame—the Safest Hiding Place

We always have to be careful not to give others the power to make us feel trapped by the positions we believe they've put us in. This is called *blame,* and it causes us to lose what little control we have over our lives.

In the earlier illustration, Martha was guilty of harboring hidden resentments toward her daughter, which eventually gave her license to blame her daughter for her feeling of being used. She was also having trouble forgiving her daughter for putting them all in this situation. She believed that forgiving her daughter meant that she was condoning her daughter's behavior. So instead, she hid her anger at her daughter behind her generosity and played the game of making the best of a bad situation.

Martha's inability to forgive made it impossible for her to let go of her anger. This in turn made her a victim of circumstance because she saw her daughter as the one to blame for ruining all of their lives.

Blaming others automatically makes us victims. This is an unattractive, yet extremely popular, way for people to lead their lives. Although many of us feel there is something to be gained by declaring ourselves victims, the gains are mostly self-defeating in the long run. Blame makes for draining and unappealing company, as we saw from Martha's closing remark.

When we play the victim, we avoid taking responsibility for our own choices and the consequences that result. Holding others accountable for our misery is a safe place to hide, but it places the responsibility for our happiness or unhappiness in someone else's hands. Personally, I recommend that we not give anyone this much control over us.

Many grandparents feel trapped under the responsibility of caring for their grandchildren. Consequently, they also feel secretly angry about being caught in a situation that is beyond their control. They resent inheriting a problem they did not create. This is only natural. But it should be a relief for us all to realize that much of the anger we feel in such a predicament is a result of how we choose to look at the situation rather than the situation itself. This means that it's within our power to be rid of it. It can be equally liberating to realize that if we're not willing or able to change a situation, changing our attitude toward it can still provide us with a much-needed sense of relief.

It takes enough precious energy to rise to the challenge of being a second-time parent. Don't waste it being angry over events that can't be reversed. Additionally, you as grandparents should understand that, depending on the circumstances, it's expected that you'll feel angry at your children when they have left you holding the bag. In effect, their bad choices become your lifelong consequences. If this is the case for you, remain very clear that the target of your anger is not your grandchildren, but the circumstance of having to raise your grandchildren. It's entirely possible for you to do this lovingly while still reserving the right to feel resentful that you have to do it at all.

If you've chosen to read this book, it's likely you already know of a grandchild in need of someone's love. True, you didn't create this child, but you either created the child who created the child, or you created the child who created the relationship that created the child.

If you have unwittingly inherited their legacy, you may find yourself cursing your children for being so irresponsible or ill-equipped as parents. Who wouldn't? You have no control over what has already been done, and fuming over it will not make it go away. Life often calls upon us to put out fires we didn't start. The fact that we didn't start them doesn't give us license to walk away and let the flames rage. In some instances, we call the act of happening upon these fires good fortune—being at the right place at the right time. If you're making yourself available to help put out this particular blaze, perhaps you, the child, and the parent should all be grateful that someone was there with a hose and the courage to use it.

But What's <u>Really</u> the Right Thing to Do?

In the interest of exploring all possible alternatives, we must consider that it is not always the best choice for grandparents to take on the commitment of raising grandchildren. Remember that "*no*" can be an answer to a prayer just as well as "*yes*." If the commitment is unmanageable, you owe it to yourself and to the child to acknowledge this, accept it, and act accordingly. Better to be honest and realistic about your limitations than to set either of you up for a lifetime of disappointment and overextended resources.

If you have come to the painful realization that you are unable to manage the responsibility of raising a grandchild, you will likely feel guilty. You may feel you have let the family down or that you've played a part in condemning an innocent child to an uncertain future. But please do remember in your soul-searching that all of our futures are equally uncertain. None of us has the long-range vision to see the distant results today's choices will have on tomorrow's plan. The best that any of us can do is to explore the benefits and drawbacks of each option we see and take whichever path seems best.

But we must also keep in mind that any choice we make should be based on a healthy balance of both reason and emotion. Don't be tempted to listen to your feelings alone. Whether you have already made your decision or are still in conflict about what to do, remember that the best choice isn't always the one that may *feel* the best. If we based all of our decisions solely on what felt the best to us, most of us would never go to work, and certainly none of us would pay our taxes! Emotion alone makes a poor advisor. If we think about it realistically, some of the best decisions we've made have been the most painful.

If you have already made the decision to take in your grandchildren, take a moment to consider what forces motivated you. Were you swayed by logic and practicality? Were you influenced by emotion? Was it all of those?

Did you base the decision in part on your need to avoid the guilt you'd feel if you had said "no," or was it because it was really the best option for everyone? Did you make the choice you made as a means of avoiding future regrets, family conflict, or the guilt others might heap on you if you had done otherwise? If you made a choice purely to avoid these kinds of uncomfortable conflicts, could it have been an unwise or self-serving one?

As humans, it's in our nature to avoid discomfort. We don't like pain. It's usually our emotions that beckon us to do what we *want* or what *feels best*.

Reason, on the other hand, teaches us that it's better to do what we *need* to do or what's *wisest* under the circumstances. Doing only what we *want* to do may feel good to us, but it will more than likely be a self-serving course of action taken only with our own needs in mind. Although it may be difficult to see an act of sacrifice or giving as having selfish motives, this can very well be, and often is, the case. Grandparents who take in their grandchildren solely because they could not face a lifetime of guilt make a choice swayed primarily by the need to avoid a painful consequence. Doing so unfortunately moves the best interest of the children to second place. We often do giving things and make sacrifices for selfish reasons without being aware that this is the case. Giving, particularly the kind of giving we're talking about here, should have no emotional strings attached.

Another important consideration in determining which choice is best in the long run is the degree of sacrifice it entails. All parents make sacrifices. It's the naive individual who believes that having children will not impact a lifestyle. People who are unwilling to make sacrifices on behalf of their children should remain childless. Unfortunately, this lack of foresight is often the very reason many grandparents find themselves raising their grandchildren...because in many cases the parents have failed to plan, prepare, consider, or accept the sacrifice involved and have proven unable or unwilling to meet the challenge. It certainly requires much less effort to *become* a parent than it does to *be* one.

It should be the willing job of any parent or parent figure to make sacrifices and to make them with love. Parents often have to go without so that their children can have the things they need. As grandparents, you may have celebrated that your days of sacrificing for the sake of your children were behind you. If you haven't yet made the decision to be a parent again, be honest with yourself in answering the question of whether you feel able and willing to make such enormous sacrifices again, particularly at this stage in your life.

If the decision has already been made and the children are already with you, it's now your challenge to expect sacrifice as part of the package, just as it was with your own children. And just as it was when you were first a parent, your time, your money, your home, your attention, your patience, and your love are once again in high demand. Again, you'll find all of these being steadily used up by the insatiable needs of a little one (or several, perhaps) who knows no end to your resources. Although you may find all of these resources stretched to the limit, you must continue to give of them freely and lovingly. If a grandparent is reluctant or begrudging in making any of these available, a feeling will be conveyed to the children that there's not enough to go around. And that may well be the truth.

That you will be stretched to your absolute limit is not in question here. However, keeping the children from being adversely affected by this reality is the true challenge of being a second-time parent. Your grandchildren should never be permitted to feel guilty about being dependent on you or for being a drain on your resources. It's the nature of being a child to do so. Nor should your grandchildren be made, whether directly or indirectly, to feel guilty about the burdens that being a second-time parent places on you. The children are no more responsible for the straits they're in than you are. You and your grandchildren are on the same team. You'll need an atmosphere of cooperation and teamwork to help maximize your combined resources instead of draining them completely.

The rigors of battle have been shown to bring soldiers together in that they share a common goal (survival) and have a common adversary (defeat). Unity among forces creates strength in times when spirits are low. Division jeopardizes everyone. If soldiers of the same army turn against one another, the enemy gains strength and will inevitably prevail. You and your grandchildren are not enemies; but when the battle heats up, it's easy to lose sight of who the enemy really is. Both you and your grandchildren will have a multitude of conflicted feelings about your predicament. The adversity you face has the power to either strengthen you or divide you, depending on how it's put to use.

Expect your grandchildren to be filled with conflicted and confusing feelings. You'll have your share as well. But as the adult, you have a responsibility to the children to have a better handle on yours. Your conflicts, doubts, confusion, resentments, and fears are not the children's problems.

Theirs, on the other hand, have now become yours. Having access to and using the help, support, and guidance you need will help you work through these emotional struggles when times are tough. (More about support in later chapters.) You can't do it all on your own. Getting help gives you strength so you can have some left over to give to your grandchildren.

Talk about Sacrifice!

As we have seen thus far, the commitment to become a parent for a second time brings with it a multitude of concerns, considerations, choices, and sacrifices. But no discussion on the subject of sacrifice would be complete without factoring in one major way in which these strains can take their toll on someone's life. Grandparents who take on the responsibility of raising their grandchildren make unimaginable sacrifices when it comes to their own lives. They put aside their goals, their careers, their relationships, their jobs, their savings, and their futures in the process. The real skill in the face of all this is for grandparents to be able to make these tremendous sacrifices freely, lovingly, and without playing the martyr. How to do this is what this section is all about.

We are all probably familiar with what is often jokingly referred to as the *martyr complex.* Perhaps we have been introduced to this idea by having been unwittingly drawn into its trap by someone playing the role of a martyr. Or maybe we are guilty of either knowingly or unknowingly having played this role ourselves. In any event, it's a common scenario that can develop under a variety of circumstances, particularly those involving giving, caretaking, or great sacrifice.

Given that the role of second-time parent is itself a commitment of ultimate sacrifice, there is a clear danger of this behavior pattern developing or carrying over here (that is, if it's not already in place). It is in this spirit that I will identify and explain the martyr personality type, discuss how it comes to be, and take a look at the potential impact it can have on all those who come in contact with it. If there are shades of the martyr in yourself or in your situation, don't be alarmed; just be willing to recognize them and do something about it. Left unattended, such a trait can not only interfere with your ability to cope but also damage already strained relationships.

First, in order to clearly understand the characteristic behaviors associated with playing the martyr, we need to understand why it's called the *martyr complex* in the first place. According to *Webster's Dictionary,* there are two applicable definitions of the word *martyr:*

1. One who endures great suffering; and

2. One who makes a great show of suffering in order to arouse sympathy.

The term *suffering* seems to be the hallmark of the martyr personality, which most of us have met at some time in our lives. Experiencing great adversity is an unavoidable consequence of living (anyone who tells you otherwise is probably trying to sell you a quick fix); however, suffering because of these hardships is a privilege reserved for the martyr alone. What the martyr fails to realize or refuses to accept is that pain is a part of living; suffering, on the other hand, is our choice. We can't avoid hardships or adversities, nor the pain that accompanies them. We can, however, avoid suffering because of them if we are willing to look for the lessons they can teach us about ourselves and the quality of the lives we are leading.

The lessons of our hardships are not immediately apparent; it is our challenge to find them. Any tragedy can reveal a hidden opportunity if placed in its proper light. Rather than viewing life's challenges as inevitable and therefore striving to make the best of them, martyrs seem to feel personally targeted for whatever difficulty befalls them. They often feel singled out, tormented, or persecuted by adversity. Some martyred individuals adopt the *"Why me?"* mentality instead of the healthier attitude of *"Why not me?"* They tend to compare their lot with others, which often leaves them feeling short-changed. They become convinced that they alone must endure more than their share of difficulty.

This is not to suggest that there is some fundamental value in pain itself but rather that pain is something we can't always avoid. In accepting that some degree of pain is a consequence of living, we take on the often formidable challenge of looking for some reason for it or of finding some meaning in it. Those who labor under the illusion that life should be free of pain are usually among the unhappiest and most dissatisfied of individuals. They live their lives either trying to avoid discomfort or searching for relief from it. When they are ultimately unsuccessful at eliminating pain, they spend the remainder of their time feeling persecuted by it.

For these individuals, their struggles serve as evidence to them that they are being unfairly put upon. This conclusion puts them in a position to feel they deserve extra credit for their heightened level of endurance. Suffering becomes a medal of valor, representative of the many battles they have been forced to fight. Displaying this medal openly, the martyr then uses it to elicit sympathy from others or to earn exemptions or special privileges. *"How could anyone expect more of someone who has already given so much?"* How could anyone be angry with or critical of someone who has endured so much adversity?

The irony hidden in this dynamic is that these individuals may curse their misfortune on one hand while inviting more calamity on the other. The danger is that they stand to either gain or lose their sense of self in their suffering. These are often individuals who lack a sense of value and merit in their own right. They earn their self-worth from their incredible tolerance for disaster and ability to function under seemingly unbearable circumstances. Whatever value they have as individuals seems to come more from what they are able to do (usually for others) than from who they are.

It's often hard to find the catch where martyrs are concerned, because they're always doing so many good deeds for others. How do we judge someone who is always putting self-interest aside to lend a helping hand? And how can we complain when everyone seems to profit from the deal: good deeds are done, and the martyr's self-worth is secured. Or is it?

Martyrs earn the image of being virtuous by giving, but the unfortunate reality is that now their value as human beings is riding on their ability to give. The balance of the scale of give and take is always tipped in their favor: the more they give, the stronger their image of being good and generous people. While it's not a bad thing to be giving, trouble comes when people begin to give and make sacrifices not because they *want* to, but because now they *have* to, just to keep up their image or maintain their self-worth.

Now let's look at how this behavior plays itself out in real-life situations. True and selfless sacrifice leaves no emotional residue. One who gives freely from the heart keeps no tally of selfless acts, nor does he or she ask for credit. In contrast, martyred giving leads to unspoken and unfulfilled expectations on the part of the giver. Because there are strings attached, this kind of giving leaves martyrs with a sense of depletion, as if they have given up something for which the recipients must feel grateful. Their actions beg to be commended, as if saying, *"Look at what I've done for you!"*

When proper credit or acknowledgment is not given to their deeds, they feel unappreciated or taken for granted. And the recipients are left with the uncomfortable feeling of having been given a gift they didn't ask for. They walk away feeling an uneasy sense of indebtedness to the giver for unsolicited generosity.

Emily

Emily is a good woman. She's well-respected by her friends and highly regarded in the community as the one you can count on when there is no one else you can count on.

Emily has just one problem: her family. It seems she's been able to command the respect and admiration of everyone else throughout her life, except her kids—and now her grandkids.

She doesn't understand it. Nor does anyone else, for that matter. In fact, her friends have been amazed at how she's managed to put up with what her kids have put her through and still play the loyal and devoted mother. And through all of her selflessness, her family seems to take no notice because they're too busy taking her for granted. But why? Isn't she just being a good mother?

When her son got fired from his job (again), who was there to take him in (again), along with his 13-year-old son and 11-year-old daughter? Emily. And when her 13-year-old grandson broke the neighbor's window, who was there to pay to have it replaced before his father found out? Emily. And when her 11-year-old granddaughter brought home a backpack that didn't belong to her, who was there to make sure the little girl it belonged to got it back? Of course, Emily.

Did anyone ever thank her? What do you think?

The problem here is that Emily's motives were all wrong. She did all these things and more not because she <u>wanted</u> to and not because it was <u>right</u>. She did them because she felt she <u>had</u> to. She so *desperately wanted her family's love and appreciation that she led herself to believe the only way to get them was to show her family how much she was willing to do for them. You see, Emily secretly believed that she didn't matter to anyone because her parents never showed her the love she needed—and she certainly wasn't going to make the same mistake with her family. So she went too far in the other direction.*

Emily believed that saying "no" to her family meant she didn't love them. So she spent all of her time making sure they had everything they wanted and needed, even to the point where she would feel horribly selfish on those odd occasions when she'd sneak home a new pair of shoes or a blouse for herself.

But instead of her tremendous self-sacrifice showing her family how devoted she was to them, it only seemed to make her out to be a doormat. Her unemployed son now ate her food, slept on her couch, watched talk shows all day on her TV, and graciously let her pay all the bills. Why? Because he could. And her grandson and granddaughter played contentedly with their video games while Emily cooked all their meals, washed all their clothes, picked up their toys, and did all the housework. Why? Because they knew she would.

So where did Emily go wrong? Her biggest mistake came in the form of her belief that being the all-devoted, all-doing, swap-meet shopping, coupon-clipping, second-hand clothes wearing, self-sacrificing martyr would earn her that sense of importance she never got from her own parents. She was doing all of this with the hidden motive of getting something back from her family: their respect, their appreciation, and their love. Because she was giving for self-serving reasons, her giving wasn't free. Every favor she did for her family (whether they asked her or not) she saw as one more favor in the bank that she thought she could cash in someday.

But that day never came. Here she was in her later years still doing everything for everyone, and on top of it all feeling bitter, resentful, and very empty inside because she'd never gotten back the one thing she really wanted. They took advantage of her because they could. It was easy.

Had someone told Emily years ago that it was okay to say "no" to the people she loved, and that surviving the rejection she feared so much would only make her stronger, she'd have been spared a lifetime of frustration.

This is by no means meant to be a judgment against anyone who has fallen into this pattern. Few set out to become martyred givers, and those who do are generally not aware of what they're doing. The way we deal with things comes from a combination of necessity and experience. We're only human, and we adapt to our circumstances in the best and most efficient ways we know how, given our individual personalities, beliefs, conditioning, and support. None of us is given a guidebook for living. In fact, it's best to look at ourselves as products of our experiences and stop passing judgment on ourselves for not knowing things we couldn't possibly have known.

Each of us interprets our world in our own unique and individual way. How we develop and adapt throughout our lives is mostly an unconscious process.

Change, on the other hand, must become a conscious process. If we are to have any hope of changing our ways of doing things, we have to first become aware of what it is we're doing. At the very least, this requires us to be honest with ourselves about what areas in our lives are in need of improvement and to be willing to take the steps to change.

Denying we need improvement robs us of an opportunity for growth. We're powerless to change what we aren't willing to see. All patterns of behavior are learned. And whatever we have learned can be unlearned and relearned in a different and more effective way.

If you have fallen into the pattern of giving and doing as an attempt to prove to yourself or others that you're an important and valuable person, your first step toward breaking this cycle is simply coming to the realization that you are doing so.

If you are unsure whether you have a tendency toward martyrdom, there are two surefire ways to find out. The first is to ask someone who knows you well and who you can trust to tell you the truth. (Remember, being completely honest with you may have been very unpleasant for this person in the past.) The second way is to take the *Martyr Test* below.

The Fifteen Warning Signs of a Martyr

Consider each of the following statements carefully. Note any that apply to you or that accurately reflect your thoughts or feelings. Identification with any of these statements is a warning sign that you may be at risk for displaying martyr-like characteristics.

The more statements you identify with, the more likely it is that you harbor unspoken expectations of those you do good deeds for.

You may be a martyr if:
❑ you find yourself doing for others things you'd rather not do just to get acceptance, appreciation, or approval from them.

❑ you have ever said, *"How could you—after all I've done for you!"*

❑ you believe that those who think of their own needs first are being selfish.

❑ you make others feel guilty when they're angry with you.

❑ you feel it's rude or disrespectful for others to disagree openly with you.

❑ you frequently feel that other people aren't pulling their weight.

❑ you do more than your share with the belief that, if left up to others, nothing would get done.

❑ you wonder why others always seem to take advantage of you or take you for granted.

❑ you find that others say and do hurtful things to you seemingly without regard for your feelings.

❑ you feel others should know what you want without you having to tell them.

❑ you feel that if others really cared about you, they'd know what you need.

❑ you often feel resentful at having to do *"everything for everyone."*

❑ you feel guilty and selfish when doing things for yourself.

❑ you put a great deal of energy into taking others' needs, wants, and feelings into consideration, and you get angry when they fail to do likewise.

❑ you feel that no one understands your pain.

If any of these statements reflect thoughts or feelings you frequently have, you may unknowingly place unspoken expectations on your relationships with family, friends, or even co-workers. Be careful not to allow these expectations to creep into your role as second-time parent.

If you've felt overburdened and unappreciated in other areas of your life, you're likely to carry this same feeling into your grandparent-grandchild relationship.

The interpersonal dynamics that are captured in the preceding statements are often set in place long before the commitment is made to take on the added responsibility of raising a second family. If you've played the martyr before, you're at risk of playing it again, unless you become aware of what you stand to gain by playing this role and what you stand to lose in giving it up. Once done, you are free to take the necessary steps to call a halt to the game.

"It just figures that I'd end up raising the kids, too! It seems all I do is clean up other peoples' messes," is a common refrain of the martyred individual. Or perhaps this one rings some bells: *"Oh, sure, I'll take care of everything. After all, no one else ever does their share."* In fact, the content of these statements may

be completely accurate, but it's their tone that drips with martyrdom. There is an angry and punishing quality about such statements. It's the underlying emotion that gives away the speaker's hidden expectations. It's these expectations that cause martyrs to lose their ability to do freely for others.

The unspoken and unfulfilled expectations are the reason for every martyr's angry tone. It's this anger that becomes generalized, clouding their ability to see a situation for what it really is. What begins as, *"I have to take care of this problem,"* quickly generalizes into, *"I have to take care of everything!"*

This tendency to exaggerate and make such broad generalizations makes it difficult for others to take martyrs seriously. It also lessens their credibility, causes others to conclude they are being overly dramatic, and discourages others from being open and honest with them. This makes martyrs feel even angrier, more disrespected, taken advantage of, and unappreciated, setting up a cycle that continues to feed on itself. People take advantage of those they don't respect and don't respect those they can take advantage of. If it has been your expectation that doing everything for everyone was the path to respect and admiration from others, you may want to think again.

An Investment In the Future

If after thorough consideration you have opted not to take on the responsibility of caring for your grandchildren, you must trust that their way will have been cleared by your honesty. After all, it takes courage to know when stepping aside is better than stepping in.

If, on the other hand, you have opted to embark on the parental journey once again, do so with love and with a healthy willingness to accept whatever assistance is available to you. It will help if you keep in mind that through all of the hardships, adversities, and seemingly insurmountable inconveniences, you and your grandchildren are on the same team and must stay united in a common goal.

In the face of all the difficulties, it's crucial for second-time parents to know where to find the rewards in their role as well as to learn to appreciate that many of these rewards will be inherent in their sacrifice. To cope with the reality of raising their children's children, grandparents have to learn to focus more on what they all stand to gain and less on what they've given up in the process. Accepting the commitment to become a parent again, if done for the right reasons, is never a loss. And the rewards are priceless: the personal satisfaction that comes from having been there for a child when no one else was; the opportunity to surround that child with love and support; and the depth of pride that comes from knowing that you were able to provide the framework for that child to discover his or her best and highest self.

The rewards of raising a second family are often subtle and elusive, but they are at the same time powerful and plentiful if you look in the right places. Whether you are now faced with the choice of being a parent all over again or you've already embarked on this journey, the following guidelines may help you uncover the rewards and be at peace with yourself, no matter what choice you've made. If you take these principles to heart, you'll find that the benefits far outnumber the heartaches and hardships.

DO NOT take on the commitment of raising a second family...

...looking for medals or trophies for your efforts or expecting a marching band to salute you for your valor.

...purely out of family obligation, which dictates that you *"should."*

...to satisfy some missing sense of purpose in your life.

...looking to prove something to yourself or others.

...to bolster a fading sense of your own purpose or self-worth.

...out of guilt or feeling that you've failed as a first-time parent.

...to satisfy an overdeveloped need to make right on where you feel you went wrong the first time.

...to compensate the child for his or her lack of a parent.

...simply to fill the void left by the child you have lost or the child who has gone astray.

...with a heavy heart and resentment for having to step into the parents' shoes.

All of these reasons carry with them a backlash that will cause aftershocks of anger, guilt, obligation, and disappointment for many years to come.

DO embrace this journey...
...out of love.
...from a genuine desire to do what is truly best for the child.
...because you can provide support, security, and a sense of belonging that is sorely lacking.
...because you are the best person for the job, with both eyes open to the joys as well as the heartaches of the experience.
...with the expectation that you will never know what *might* have happened had you not been there and chosen to do so.
...with the understanding that you will bring emotional baggage of your own to the experience, but with it you'll also bring the willingness to work it through.
...with pride that you had the courage and integrity to put aside self in order to do what was right and in the best interest of another human being.

And most importantly, *do* appreciate that, although this is a difficult and demanding road, you never have to lose sight of the precious and unique opportunities it can bring. You are making an investment in the future, an important investment that with love, patience, and courage can yield a windfall beyond your wildest imagination.

Love is a priceless gift that can't be fully realized until it's given away. A grandparent's love is a special kind of love that springs from a reservoir deep within the soul. With the proper understanding and support, this love, when given, does not leave a sense of depletion, but rather a sense of fulfillment known only to those who have traveled this way.

$$3$$

"Where Did J Go Wrong?"

Let's face it, if things were as they should be, grandparents would have no responsibility for raising their grandchildren. So when grandparents *do* heed the call, it's only because things are *not* as they should be. And although they may not be ashamed of their new status, most grandparents do the job only because they care deeply for the little people who are in harm's way.

Also, they don't do it for the purpose of raising their own self-esteem. Rather, this commitment is one they take on with a heavy heart and a deeply felt sense of family loyalty. And as if to make matters even worse, many grandparents are haunted by the feeling that in some way they're to blame— that their child's inability to rise to the challenge of being a parent is actually their fault.

If you are like many grandparents, *"Where did I go wrong?"* may be the single question that has most often nagged at your conscience and disrupted your sleep. It's this overwhelming sense of feeling in some way personally responsible for their grandchildren's predicament that leads grandparents to also feel responsible for making it better.

If you as a grandparent blame yourself for your adult child's unwillingness or inability to provide for his or her own child, you may be one of those grandparents who uses caring for the grandchildren as a means of making up for where you feel you've gone wrong as a parent yourself. The danger is, if you're already feeling guilty and inadequate, doing this may set you up to take responsibility for fixing things that aren't your responsibility to fix—things that will only set you up to feel more guilty and even more inadequate in the long run.

As a grandparent with grandchildren at home, it's impossible for you to escape the daily reality of what happens when a parent is absent or uninvolved in a child's life. And as a grandparent raising grandchildren, you also cannot escape the constant and sometimes poignant reminders of the true toll that absence can take on a child.

If being the living witness to this tragedy makes you feel guilty about the situation your family is in, then these daily images will take on new meaning for you. For you, they're more than just the day-to-day problems a family faces; they've become a constant reminder of your shortcomings as a parent. Consumed by guilt, you see the problems around you as proof that you need to fix things in a desperate attempt to prove to yourself and to the world that you're making right where you feel you've gone wrong.

It's entirely possible for a grandparent who is caught in this maze of guilt and responsibility to do all the right things for all the wrong reasons. The end result may be that everyone is taken care of, but the emotional toll on the grandparent caregiver is hardly worth the cost.

Removing the added burden of blaming yourself may not reduce the pressures you face as a grandparent, but it can certainly make the reality of the pressures you feel a bit easier to bear. Chances are, some of your actions may very well have contributed to your present situation, but chances are equally good that you're not to *blame* for nearly as much as you fear. You'll feel much better about the outcome if you learn to *understand* what part you and others may have played in creating the whole situation instead of assigning blame.

Understanding gives you the ability to learn from your mistakes, it allows you to forgive yourself and others for being imperfect, and it lets you put these mistakes to use by making changes in the here and now. *Blame* only serves to fill you with negative feelings. It makes you do things for others to relieve your guilt, and it makes others feel that they have to do things for you to make up to you for letting you down. We all make mistakes—we just have to make good on them. *Blame* makes a waste of perfectly good mistakes.

If you are a grandparent hopelessly sinking in the mire of guilt, easy does it—there is help ahead. By merely adjusting some of your old ideas, you can be relieved of much of the unnecessary guilt you've piled on yourself. This in turn will lighten your overall load, freeing you to face your family problems with dignity instead of shame.

It seems that grandparents in general have a number of basic misconceptions regarding family roles and responsibilities that cause them to feel guilty when there is really no need to. These misconceptions translate into three very common mistakes. Grandparents will:

1. Try to protect their grandchildren from seeing the parent's shortcomings or feeling the parent's absence by trying to replace the parent
2. Take the grandchildren's emotional struggles personally, feeling it means that they as grandparents are not doing a good enough job of filling the void
3. Try to control the child's impression of the parent or relationship with the parent by inserting themselves in between the parent and the child

As you will see, these actions are taken with the best of intentions at heart, but they can serve to make an already difficult situation even worse. Each of these efforts will only leave grandparents feeling that they can't win, no matter what they do. And finally, being caught in this kind of a no-win situation will only add to a grandparent's tendency toward guilt and self-blame.

Each of these three areas is explored in more detail in the three sections that follow.

1. The case of the replaceable parent

No one could easily deny that the single most significant relationship any of us will ever have is the one we have (or don't have) with our parents. If you are a grandparent trying your best to fill a parent's shoes, don't lose sight of this fact.

Parents and grandparents are not interchangeable parts of a child's life. Your willingness to serve as stand-in on behalf of your grandchildren is noble and admirable, but don't attach magical powers to your efforts. No matter how valiant these efforts may be, they'll never have the power to protect your grandchildren from the void left by the absence of a parent. So don't blame yourself for the pain your grandchildren are bound to go through, but rather understand that their pain is a necessary reaction to their loss.

Don't take their pain or their struggles to mean that you're not doing a good enough job or that they're ungrateful or unappreciative of your efforts. No matter how you look at it, having a grandparent as a stand-in for a parent is not natural. That's not the way it's supposed to be.

So then, if we're in agreement that the parent-child relationship is the most significant relationship we'll ever have, and if we accept that not even a best-intentioned grandparent can make the substitution, then the next series of questions you'll ask is quite clear: *"How is a child affected by the loss or absence of a parent?"* *"How is a child affected by a parent's inability to cope with the pressures of just being a parent?"* *"Will the parent's abuse, neglect, or inconsistency leave permanent scars?"* But what you'll most want to know is, *"How can I keep this from happening?"*

We can say with reasonable certainty that such factors will have an impact on a child, but no one can really say how or to what extent. Although we can't deny that the quality of our relationship with our parents plays a major role in setting the tone for the person we'll later become, we have to be realistic. Having a healthy parent-child bond is undeniably good for the mind and the soul, but not having one doesn't necessarily doom an individual to a lifetime of self-indulgent misery. It certainly *can* be devastating for children to have inconsistent or nonexistent emotional ties to their parents, but it doesn't *have* to be. What makes the difference is how each child is helped to adjust—which, in turn, falls at least in part on the shoulders of the grandparents.

With all this in mind, understand that when your grandchildren's changing moods and unpredictable temperament begin to play on your last remaining nerve, what you may be witnessing is just a child's natural reaction to the inability to establish a meaningful link with the most meaningful person in his or her life. It will help you to replace exasperation with understanding if you can reach back into your fading memory and recall that you, too, were once a child in need of a parent's love, acceptance, and understanding. If you had trouble getting those, you may well have come just a little bit closer to understanding what your grandchild is going through.

To more fully appreciate just how powerful and longlasting a child's need for a parent's love can be, consider for a moment the relationship you've had with your own parents. Was it all you wanted it to be? How did your relationship with them change as you moved from childhood through adolescence and into adulthood? Are they still in your life? Have your feelings toward them changed as you've grown older and gained more life experience? How have they contributed to the person you are today? Do they continue to contribute to that person?

What lessons have you learned from their mistakes or experiences that may have helped to shape the person you've become? Have you lived up to their expectations of you, or do you feel you've disappointed them in some way? Do you feel you've made good on the things they've done for you, or have you had to work extra hard to make up for what they weren't able to do?

Now take a few more moments to reflect a bit more closely on the quality of your relationship with your parents, particularly during your critical early years. Was it close or distant? Cold or loving? Punishing or nurturing? Accepting or rejecting? Comfortable or strained? If your bond was strong, think about what it might have been like to have had that bond suddenly taken from you. If your bond was shaky, how did that affect the way you felt about yourself? How have you been able to deal with life's troubles and changes without the support you needed? If another person had to step in to give you what your parents could not, did this take your mind off the fact that your parents couldn't be counted on?

If you lost a parent or were abandoned by one, no one knows better than you the depth of this childhood pain. If your relationship with your parents was stormy, then your experience connects you more closely with your grandchildren's feelings than anything else. The painful truth for your grandchildren, as it may have been for you, is that there is no quick fix for this kind of heartache. Having an indifferent parent hurts. Not having a parent in your life at all hurts even more. As the grandparent, you can help to soothe this ache and begin the healing process; but face it, no matter how devoted you are, you simply can't make it go away.

Many grandparents cannot bear to see the hurt their grandchildren go through over the loss of a parent (keeping in mind that the parent need not have died for there to still be a sense of loss). These grandparents have enough on their minds just dealing with their own feelings, let alone having to ease the pain of their grandchildren as well. Painful as it may be for them all, the children have to be allowed to freely express the wide range of feelings their situation is bound to bring up. Don't do yourself the injustice of believing that if you were doing a good enough job, your grandchildren wouldn't feel badly that their parents aren't there.

Brandi

*"Mum-mum, are you mad because I call you "Mum-mumí?"
Brandi asked.*

"Of course not, honey," her grandmother answered. "Why would you think I'd be mad?"

"Because my mom says I shouldn't call you that. She says it sounds too much like I'm calling you 'Mama.' She says it makes her think I love you better than her."

"You can call me anything you want, Brandi," her grandmother reassured. "It doesn't mean I'm taking your mother's place or that you love her any less."

"But she says you're trying to make me love you more, and that's why you want me to call you 'Mum-mum.' She says you're trying to take me away from her."

"Honey, your mother will always be your mother, and what you call me will never change that. You can have room in your heart for me, and still have plenty left for her..."

"But she says that's why she doesn't come around much. She says if I want you to be my mom, then she should stay out of it."

"Well," the grandmother paused, "it sounds to me like she's really afraid we don't need her anymore. Sometimes when we feel like people don't need us, we stay away just to teach them a lesson. Don't worry, it's not your fault. She's just having trouble understanding that you won't forget about her just because you're with me now."

Your valiant and courageous efforts alone won't be enough to fill the void left by the absent parents. You may very well be much more the parent in your grandchildren's lives than their parents ever were or ever will be, but you are not, and cannot ever replace the missing parents. Trying to do so is a losing battle. In the end, you will feel not only that you've failed as a parent but that you've failed as a grandparent as well. Spare yourself this anguish.

Not only can you not replace a parent, you can't effectively make a child forget that the parent isn't there. Many grandparents set themselves up for more pain by believing that if they play the parental part convincingly enough, their grandchildren will forget about the disappointment the absent parent is causing them and look to the grandparent to give them what the missing parent cannot.

The truth is, you couldn't create a diversion to make them forget about their parents, and the love and acceptance you provide, no matter how deep, just isn't the same. So, avoid giving your grandchildren the idea that you are their newly appointed parent. You'll only end up feeling rejected and unappreciated when your wise grandchildren become angry with you for thinking they could be so easily fooled.

Families, like engines, can run quite smoothly with substitute parts; but, unlike engines, they don't run as well. Needless to say, you as the substitute part may function far better in your capacity than the original, but you are a substitute, just the same. Be realistic with your expectations of yourself and with your grandchildren's ability to adjust to the changes and disruptions in their lives. Assuming the role of parent in name as well as in status can inadvertently give your grandchildren the idea that you're telling them, *"Forget about your mom and dad."* Having been a child yourself once, oh so long ago, you know that this just isn't possible.

Our need to connect with our parents is an inescapable consequence of being human. The absence of this connection leaves children and adults alike with a lifelong heartache. It's human to long for and to seek out the answer to that most fundamental question, *"Where did I come from?"*

For some, the more important question is, *"Where did it all go wrong?"* Children of troubled or disinterested parents often feel it's their fault and are left longing for a kind of reassurance their parents simply may not be able to give. Unwilling to give up the hope (or in some cases, the fantasy) of having that close parent-child relationship, these children continue long into adulthood setting themselves up for more hurt and disappointment by trying to find just the right thing to say or do that will at long last win them their parents' approval. Without help and understanding, children of these kinds of parents become lost in the belief that they simply aren't deserving of the parents' love. For them, life can easily become a self-defeating quest to answer the unanswerable question, *"What could I have possibly done to be rejected by my own parents?"*

Simply stated, children need parents, not substitutes. And children of negligent or self-centered parents are put in the unfortunate position of needing the very thing they may never be able to get. As the substitute in this case, you as the grandparent have to get comfortable with being second-best. No matter how ill-equipped or unsuitable the parents may be in your informed opinion—no matter how much of a liability they may seem to be in your grandchildren's lives—the need for their love will always come first. Being abandoned, abused, or rejected never stopped a child from wanting a parent's love.

Just as certainly as you can expect your grandchildren to feel resentful of, and abandoned by, their parents, you can expect them to long for, idealize, and even defend those same parents. It's very common for children to pass through a wide range of phases over time, swinging from hating their parents to loving them, as their feelings and ability to understand their situation change. At times, children may even seem to switch between emotions literally from one moment to the next as they wrestle with the conflict between what they want and what they really have. Don't try to figure it out—their feelings (like ours) defy logic. You'd be best to brace yourself for riding out these emotional ups and downs by being patient and by administering generous doses of good, old-fashioned understanding. Avoid taking their emotional extremes too seriously, and understand that such changes in mood, although surprising, are never permanent.

The most important insight you have to offer your grandchildren as they weather the storm of conflicted feelings is perhaps a lesson you've just learned yourself without even realizing you'd learned it. Namely, that whatever your parents' shortcomings may be, don't take them personally. In life, as we gain maturity and experience, most of us will also gain the wisdom to understand that when someone isn't capable of giving us what we need, it doesn't mean we're not deserving of it. And parents are no exception. Parents, as we know all too well, are simply people who have children. No astonishing feat there! Anyone with the right biological makeup can accomplish that. And, just like the rest of us, parents are subject to the same limitations they have always had. At this stage of your life, it's likely that you're coming to the realization that you have to accept yourself in spite of your shortcomings and stop beating yourself up for the mistakes you've made because of them. Following this same rule, you must also be willing to accept the shortcomings of others.

The most important thing you can help your grandchildren to understand is that, although their parents may not be able to show them the kind of love they need, it doesn't mean they're unlovable. If children learn early that their parents' limitations are their parents' problems and not their own, they can be spared a lifetime of self-doubt—and they just might avoid the misery of trying to find that love and acceptance in all the wrong places. With help, these children can come to understand that the distance separating them from their parents is a result of their parents' inability to be sensitive or to give their children what they need and is not a statement about what the children deserve.

To be able to show love, we have to first be able to receive it. Both giving and receiving require a kind of openness and vulnerability that some are just not capable of achieving. Our ability to be sensitive to others or to be accepting or understanding of them is determined by how open we are to them. To be loving, we have to feel loved, and to feel loved, we have to believe we are worth loving. If we felt unloved as children, we may become adults unable to openly express love. If we don't have enough love for ourselves, how can we expect to have any left over for others? Simply put, we can't give away what we simply haven't got. Those who believe that finding someone to care for will make them more lovable are only fooling themselves.

If we feel in our hearts that we're not worth loving, our giving or loving acts become hollow, forced, and self-serving. The same principle applies to you as a grandparent. As we've said before, if your parental guilt has manifested itself in your grandparental caregiving, it's probable that you can be doing all the right things for all the wrong reasons. You deserve better for yourself.

2. *Good parent...bad parent...grandparent*

When we fully appreciate the significance of the parent-child relationship, we can understand more clearly why children often resist seeing their parents' faults. It's just less traumatic for children to blame themselves, circumstances, other people, and in this case, even you, for their parents' absence than it is to believe that their parents either don't want them or can't take care of them. As they struggle to find stability in their unstable worlds, it's necessary for children to keep their parents in a place of high regard. If they can't count on the very people responsible for their existence, who *can* they count on? It may defy logic, but it's not unusual for some children, even in the face of obvious evidence, to refuse to believe that their parents have failed them.

This being the case, children are more likely to blame themselves for their parents' absence or abandonment than to see their parents as being at fault. Children simply have less to lose in seeing themselves as flawed than their parents—if their parents are flawed, children lose the most basic stability they'll ever hope to have.

If you find yourself becoming frustrated or even angry when your grandchildren begin to speak favorably about the self-same parent who has wronged you both so badly, remind yourself that it's your own outrage and bitter experience that makes you feel you have the responsibility to set the record straight. Bite your tongue and trust that time and their own experience will set the record straight, on their own terms and in their own time.

With this in mind, expect that your grandchildren's ideas about their parents will be very different from yours. This is only natural. You've had more experience and a much longer history with the parents than the children have. Given your differing vantage points, it would only make sense that you would draw different conclusions about the same people.

As a grandparent in a tough situation, it's vital that you let these differences in opinion be. Understand that your grandchildren's point of view may be inaccurate or incomplete, but it's not *wrong*. If you look at their impressions as *"wrong,"* you'll feel obliged to *"correct"* them. An abbreviated version of a novel is not *"wrong,"* it is just incomplete—there are pieces missing.

What your grandchildren have done is formed an equally valid opinion based on a more limited set of facts. The same story read from different starting points is bound to leave a different impression on the reader. Your grandchildren have started the story in the middle, but that doesn't give you the right or the responsibility to fill in the rest of it for them. Be patient and allow them to catch up at their own pace and on their own terms. By allowing them to do so, you give them the opportunity to reach a conclusion that's meaningful to them, instead of one you've given them because you were too impatient to wait for them to catch up on their own.

Grandparents caring for grandchildren would do well to stay out of the middle when it comes to forming the children's opinions about their parents. You can't win here. Remember, developing an accurate impression of any person is a process and not an event. Trust the process.

Libby

Brandi's grandmother, Libby, sat in her weekly support group meeting. "You told her what?" one of the other grandparents exclaimed. "You told Brandi her mother was just feeling left out! I'd have told her she's lucky you even let her mother come around at all!"

"Why would I want to tell her a thing like that?" Libby asked.

"After what she's done to Brandi, I don't see how you can keep your mouth shut. Your daughter's done nothing but hurt her...she deserves to feel left out!"

"But Brandi loves her," Libby replied. "Why would I want to hurt her even more by running her mother's name into the ground?"

"But she doesn't know the whole story, Libby!" the grandfather fumed. "How can you sit back and let her mother sweet-talk her like that? You're playing right into her hand. You're too soft! I'd set that kid straight in no time!"

"Well," Libby sighed, "that's where you and I disagree. My daughter has more problems than Brandi can understand at this point, and I refuse to add to them by taking away what little her mother gives her. I can't understand why you insist that it's manipulation that Brandi thinks so much of her. I think it's good she still has that to hold on to."

The grandfather stood his ground. "Well, I told my grandson that he's better off without his dad around. I'm not afraid to tell him the truth. I don't think we should candy-coat any of this for them. My son sure didn't think about what it would do to his son the night he killed that guy, so why should I worry about what my grandson thinks about him?"

Libby wasn't so willing to back down, either. "Your situation is different. What Brandi learns about her mother I think should come from her own experience. I agree with you that I shouldn't protect her from the truth, but I also don't believe in telling her stuff she *hasn't seen yet herself just because I don't agree with what her mother's done."*

For most children in the care of their grandparents, the extent of the relationship they have with their parents will consist of periodic visits and random contacts. This inconsistency appears to work in the parents' favor because it allows them to show their children only the side of themselves they want them to see. Parents who spend little time with their children enjoy a distinct advantage in that they develop a biased or one-dimensional relationship with them (sometimes called the *Disneyland Dad* syndrome). Because they are able to control what their children see of them, it's easy for them to save their best for these occasions. Even the most disturbed person can pull off an appearance of having it together for short periods of time. Only experience, consistency, time, and frequency of contact can wear down a person's facade and expose the real person underneath. Don't be too eager to tear down this facade for the benefit of your grandchildren. They will only resent you for it.

Unfortunately, in saving their best for their children, these parents can too easily save their worst for you. Sadly, struggles over money, custody, visitation, responsibility, and control are common scenes between parents and grandparents. Simple in principle but difficult in practice, the struggles between you and the parents should stay there. If they are able to save the very best of themselves for their children, it might be difficult for you, but you'll need to find a way to be grateful for this. If the parents' ability to show different faces to you and their children seems manipulative, so be it. If the children benefit in some small way from this, your challenge is to gracefully step aside and allow it to happen. Don't get caught up in feeling that the parents are manipulating the children in order to turn them against you. If you interfere with this process, you'll be just as guilty of manipulating the children against their parents.

Even if you can't control whether the parents play the children against you, you can do the responsible thing and avoid playing the same game. Your grandchildren should never pay for the conflicts you have with their parents. If you damage the children's impression of their parents because of your experience, you take something away from them just because of their parents' misdeeds. Don't be so quick to take away what little positive the children may get from their parents out of your fear that they'll be fooled and reject you after all you've done. This rarely happens, and when it does, it usually doesn't last long.

You as the grandparent perform a delicate balancing act when it comes to the parent-child relationship. Not only do you have to avoid making the parents out to be faultless, but at the same time, you have to avoid filling the children's ears with unnecessary negativity. You have to stay neutral and trust that time, age, and experience on their own will allow your grandchildren to form a complete and accurate picture. Your grandchildren will later have to decide for themselves whether or not there's a relationship there worth saving.

You may not be able to enjoy the immediate payoff that goes along with being that part-time parent or *Disneyland Mom/Dad*, but it's the rare child who doesn't eventually come to appreciate who has been more the parent and understand who has really been there the whole time.

3. The family tug-of-war...Who are you pulling for?

Not only do grandparents inherit the challenge of not interfering with their grandchildren's relationship with their parents, but they also have to avoid covering up or making excuses in an effort to force a relationship between parent and child.

Some grandparents may even find themselves working harder than the parent to keep some contact going between parent and child. They spend valuable time arranging contacts and setting up visits the parent just isn't interested in. Believe that, if the parent and the child are to have any relationship at all, it will happen in spite of you, not because of you.

Rather than investing your precious time and attention making up for and excusing a parent's lack of involvement, it may be better for you to concentrate on helping your grandchildren understand and cope with it. You can't force a parent to be more involved in a child's life, but you *can* help your grandchildren learn to enjoy a rich and fulfilling life in the shadow of this reality.

It's natural for grandparents to become angry when their grandchildren speak favorably of the parent who has let them all down. But when children speak favorably about what the parent has done for them or with them, this is not a rejection of you or your efforts. It is truly dedicated grandparents who can sit quietly in the background while their grandchildren rave about the time they've spent with the parent who has hurt, disappointed, and betrayed them all so deeply.

It's entirely possible, and even probable, that parents, however manipulative, verbally abusive, or out of control in your experience, can be consistently warm and loving toward their own children. You as the designated protector of the children will need to keep your eyes open, but be objective about this. Be certain to judge how the parents interact with the children separately from the way they interact with you. It's often the case that parents who refuse to cooperate with the grandparents are able to maintain a relatively positive, if not inconsistent, relationship with their own children.

This inconsistency can make the struggle over visitation a complex and uncomfortable one for grandparent caregivers. As long as these children are in your care, you are the primary care provider and have responsibility for assessing any potentially damaging situations in order to protect your grandchildren from harm. Because this burden falls on you, you as the grandparent caregiver have the right to determine with whom the children are permitted to spend time, even when it comes to their own parents.

Of course, this doesn't give you free reign to deny the parents access without good reason simply because you're angry or need to show them who's in control. But you do have a right to determine if spending time with their parents could put the children in harm's way. This often leaves the door open for an ugly power struggle between parent and grandparent. The very same parents who trust you to protect their children from harm will become instantly hostile and vindictive if you deem then to be one of those potential threats.

Of course, such problematic incidents could be cleanly re-solved by placing them in the hands of impartial third parties such as arbitrators or judges. But most grandparents raising grandchildren are reluctant to invite these authorities into their family disputes. Some avoid taking this route because they're intimidated by the size and complexity of *"the system,"* or simply because they can't afford an attorney to walk them through the maze of legalities. Others know that in the deep and unforgiving vacuum that is our legal system, the voices of grandparents are weak and more than likely won't be heard.

So this leaves the lion's share of scuffling over custody, guardianship, financial support, visitation, and control to take place at home.

Because of their lack of real clout, grandparents then find themselves afraid to take a strong stand and will back down even when it's against their better judgment. If they prohibit parents from spending time with their children, the parents could threaten to take legal action. If this happens, the grand-parents risk losing their grandchildren altogether. So, unless these children are in clear danger, they remain subject to the parents' whims when it comes to visits and frequency or infre-quency of contact.

As the grandparent, you certainly don't have the power to make a parent more responsible or more able to manage his or her life. Nor can you make a parent more able or willing to take an active role in his or her children's lives. You can't make a parent spend quality time with a child, but what you must do at all times is stay alert to the kinds of interactions the parent has with the child during the time they do spend to-gether. Regardless of how effective or ineffective the parent has proven to be in managing personal affairs, your focus must remain on whether the parent is capable of securing the child's safety and well-being when they're together. Don't allow the parent to bully you into taking your grandchildren into a po-tentially dangerous environment—but at the same time, be careful not to protect them from a threat that might not exist. Although unpleasant, being exposed to a parent who is lazy, immature, unreliable, or irresponsible is not in itself damaging. These should only be of concern when they prevent the parent from being able to make sound judgments with regard to the child's safety and overall well-being.

Furthermore, you alone do not have the capacity to compensate your grandchildren for having an absent or indifferent parent. The biggest influence you'll have in your surrogate parent role is in helping your grandchildren cope with and accept this painful reality. We all learn at some point in our lives that things are not always the way we'd like them to be. Our true road to mental health and happiness is paved with the realization that it is our challenge to craft the best product from whatever raw materials life has given us.

You weren't the one who chose the raw materials your grandchildren were given, so don't blame yourself for how little they got or designate yourself the master carpenter who will make sure these materials are expertly put to use. No matter how poor the quality of these materials may seem to be, it will ultimately be for your grandchildren to decide the kind of life they will build with them. You can provide them with the tools, but you can't decide for them how they'll use those tools.

As the guardian, protector, and spokesperson for your grandchildren, you certainly *do* have the power to create a protective environment where you model for them the principles and philosophies you believe in until they're old enough and mature enough to decide for themselves whether or not they'll choose to make them their own. If you do this to the best of your ability and your grandchildren go on to make poor decisions in their later lives or they choose to stay angry or bitter because they didn't have the most perfect childhood, rest assured that this has not been your doing. Just as your parents helped lay the foundation on which you later built your life, you will be no more responsible for your grandchildren's triumphs than you will be to blame for their tragedies. If you have done your best to encourage them to make the most of their lives in spite of their hardships, your job is done. The rest is up to them.

The final step in the process of relieving yourself of guilt and finally shedding the blanket of blame is for you to forgive yourself for not being a perfect parent. Remember that, no matter what mistakes you may have made as a parent, your children, and eventually your grandchildren, will be responsible for the choices they will go on to make as adults.

Perhaps your adult children blame you for their poor life choices, claiming that you didn't properly prepare them to manage the pressures of life. Perhaps this is at least in part the truth. And perhaps the guilt you feel over this has made you its prisoner and has made it impossible for you to shift the responsibility back to where it really belongs—on them. It's easy to be drawn into the trap of taking the blame, but it's now time for you to climb out of that trap and free your adult children to take responsibility for themselves.

The fact is, no one can heap on you more responsibility than you're willing to accept. If your adult children have appointed you the clean-up crew for their calamities and you have willingly obliged, you have played a part in your own undoing. But realize now (even if after the fact) that *their* gain from this arrangement has been far greater than *yours*. You have little to lose by resigning this position. In so doing, you will free yourself to approach your role as second-time parent as a necessary challenge and not just another one of their messes they've elected you to clean up.

This cycle of blame and responsibility is a powerful and destructive one that goes like this: as a parent, you take responsibility for your adult child's life, and they in turn blame you when things go wrong. This causes you to feel guilty for doing the wrong thing, which makes you feel obligated to make it right. This only sets you up to be blamed when it all goes wrong again. Sound familiar?

The more responsibility you assume, the less they will. In the end, your efforts are unappreciated, and you feel used. You *have* been.

As we've said before, others take advantage of those they don't respect and don't respect those they can take advantage of. In the interest of gaining approval or appreciation by doing for others, we often overstep our bounds and do more than we should (or, at least more than we're asked to). We set ourselves up to be used, and in the end we have lost the respect we thought we were earning. Beware of how much responsibility you are willing to take for others. Your efforts will backfire horribly if you overdo it.

If you as a grandparent feel unappreciated and used, or resentful that your adult children, now parents themselves, have yet again set you up to bail them out of a fix they've gotten themselves into, your anger in this matter is justified. But the painful truth may be that your willingness to bail them out has contributed to their overall failure to become responsible adults.

This is not to say that you are to blame for the situation you're now in; it's merely an acknowledgment that some of your anger may be aimed at yourself for having allowed this to happen in the first place.

If this is the case, remember, the mud is never too deep, and it's never too late to begin crawling out of it. Your children may have fallen short in taking responsibility as parents, thus leading you to step in. But it's past time for you to at last begin stepping back and allowing them to make their own way, their own plans, and their own mistakes on the journey to becoming responsible adults.

You may not have known in your earlier years, but you do understand now, that you can choose whether to become a *caretaker* or a *caregiver*. A caretaker is one who does for others what they could otherwise do for themselves. The caregiver, on the other hand, is simply one who does for others what they aren't able to do for themselves.

All children need caretakers, but with the proper balance of knowing when to step in and when to step aside, all children should eventually outgrow their need for one. When the caregiver's actions begin to keep people from learning how to do for themselves, the caregiver becomes a caretaker. (It's okay to bite the hand that feeds you when it keeps you from feeding yourself.)

With this in mind, you are at long last free to decide between investing your energy in necessary action and appropriate responsibility or in avoidable blame. Instead of asking, *"Where did I go wrong?"* It's time to start asking, *"What am I going to do about it now?"*

4

Where Have All the Parents Gone?

Any number of circumstances can create the shift in family structure that places a grandchild in the care of a grandparent. What most of these cases have in common is the absence or inability of the parent to adequately provide for the care of a child.

When the parent is missing, the grandparents step into the generational space where the parent should be. In some cases, the grandparents temporarily fill this space, such as when the parent is disabled, incarcerated, hospitalized, or involved in treatment of some kind. In other cases, the grandparents must step in permanently to act as surrogate parents when the parent has died or has simply abandoned the child altogether. And in still other more confusing situations, the parent remains actively involved in the child's life (or even in the home) but turns over primary responsibility for the care of the child to the grandparents. In many of these cases, it's never really clear whether the child will remain permanently in the care of the grandparents or at some point will return to the care of the parent. In each of these circumstances, the balance and structure of the entire family unit is changed.

When a parent is absent, the grandparent takes over the role of parent, thus inheriting the uncomfortable task of parenting a child who is one generation removed. When the parent merely steps aside and the grandparent steps in, the generational order is disrupted and the customary family roles are reassigned. Instead of the parent being in the pivotal position between grandparent and grandchild, the grandparent now assumes the difficult and delicate position between parent and child. With loyalties and emotional investments on either side of this balance, the grandparent sits between parent and child, bearing the weight of each set of loyalties like the ends of a seesaw. And like the balancing seesaw, the grandparent has to find a comfortable resting place midway between parent and child, knowing that if personal loyalties shift too far to one side or the other, the equilibrium of the new family structure will be lost. Maintaining this position for any length of time is exhausting.

In any circumstance in which grandparent and grandchild are brought together in this manner, the grandparent faces some unique and even bewildering challenges. Each specific case carries with it its own unique set of obstacles, but in all cases, the grandparents are left to discover their own emotional balance while finding strength enough to become a guiding force for a troubled child who needs answers, support, and direction.

The remainder of this chapter is divided into three subsections, each tackling the challenges that result from the three most common reasons children end up in their grandparents' care. Section one offers help and support for both grandparents and grandchildren grieving the death of a parent. The second section deals with the problem of the addicted parent. The final portion sifts through the emotional fallout of the unpredictable or unreliable parent.

Picking Up the Pieces: When a Parent Dies

The challenges facing families who must pick up the pieces after losing a loved one are substantial. It is often agreed that there is no pain greater for a parent than to lose a child, no matter the age—this simply defies the natural and expected order of things. It can be likewise said that there must be no pain deeper for a child than to lose a parent. For grandparents who inherit the care of their grandchildren in the aftermath of a parent's death, the tragedy is twofold; the grandparents are left to mourn the loss of their own child while simultaneously struggling to comfort a child who is grieving the loss of a parent.

For these grandparents, caring for their grandchildren can often provide a well-needed respite from the pain. As they weather the crisis together, grandparent and grandchild cling to one another, finding some comfort and relief in the warmth of each other's embrace. The depth of their shared sorrow bonds them together in the realization that they will need one another's strength to hold the family together and to keep from falling apart.

In such events, both grandparent and grandchild will need help navigating the painful process of coming to terms with their loss. Both will undoubtedly experience their share of the conflicting emotions such a loss brings, from anger to guilt, from depression to denial. It's important for everyone to understand that mourning is a process that is experienced by each person in his or her own way over widely varying periods of time. Managing one's own grief is often more than enough, but helping a child in doing the same can be too much for even a brave and levelheaded grandparent to bear.

Overwhelmed by feelings, grandparents may dive headlong into the parental role, making it their mission to compensate the entire family for their loss. In holding such high expectations for themselves, grandparents may take on the heavy burden of trying to replace the missing parent as an alternative to facing the painful reality of the empty space they all share. Becoming preoccupied with taking care of the routine business of providing for the children creates such a healing distraction that no one even notices that it's slowly become an all-out effort to stave off the surging tide of pain.

Unable to face the finality of such a loss, grandparents become increasingly caught up in the day-to-day business of keeping the family afloat. The hitch in this plan is that, when covered up, the pain of any loss doesn't go away; it gets buried underneath all the distractions. Unfortunately, because the feelings are trapped, the healing process gets lost in the emotional shuffle.

Any loss, particularly the loss of a close family member, is a devastating blow for anyone. But however excruciating the pain may be, the feelings must be given free expression. Pushing these feelings aside in the interest of *"being strong for the family"* may provide temporary relief, but it can create long-term problems if such efforts become habitual. Avoidance tactics serve only to cover up the wound, hiding it from view while it continues to fester underneath. Only if it is uncovered and exposed to the air will the wound eventually be allowed to heal.

Both grandparent and grandchild must have the opportunity to discuss their feelings about such a significant loss freely and openly. This often requires professional help in the form of counseling or support groups. These avenues offer a safe and open place to sort through powerful feelings without the added concern of burdening one another with their sadness. Counseling and other professional support can also take the burden off the grandparents or other family members who feel they have to find the right things to say or do to comfort one another and ease their pain.

In such situations, it's only natural for family members to make attempts to comfort or console each other with kind words and soothing phrases. But in so doing, we have to pay attention to the subtle messages our attempts at comfort may really convey. We use sympathetic statements like, *"Everything will be all right,"* or, *"She is in a better place now,"* without even thinking because they're the standard fare in times of grief. But without intending to, such phrases and others like them can minimize the magnitude of a person's pain.

The message others (especially children) may really hear in these expressions is, *"Don't feel so bad."* The finality of death brings up feelings of helplessness in us all. If we could only do something to help...but, alas, we can't. So this helplessness makes us resort to those expressions, which satisfy our need to feel that we've actually done something to help. In reality, these types of expressions do more to satisfy our own need to feel helpful than they do the grieving person's need to be helped. Sometimes the best we can offer people in their time of mourning is to recognize our own helplessness and allow them the dignity of their pain. There's nothing wrong with saying, *"I wish I had some words that could ease your pain,"* or, *"There's nothing I could possibly say that would make you feel any better."*

This lets people know that we're all helpless and allows them the full depth of grief without feeling guilty or judged.

No one has ever been known to successfully lift a grieving person's sorrow with clichés alone. No one should. This fact holds true for grieving children as well as adults. Clichés do little to lessen the depth of such a tragedy, but we can't help but throw them out there like life preservers because we haven't got anything else to offer. We fear that if we don't throw them something, they'll drown...or, are we really afraid that if we don't offer something to make them feel better, their sorrow will drown us?

By saying things like, *"It'll be okay,"* we're making a desperate attempt to plug up the hole in the dam before it breaks. Could we really handle the full depth of another person's sorrow? Be careful of whose best interests you're really looking out for, and choose your words accordingly.

There are others who deal with death simply by refusing to deal with it. But acting as if it never happened is just as unhealthy as trying to erase the pain with kind words. The fact of the matter is that grief won't vanish under the cloak of denial. Even worse than avoidance or distraction, the refusal to even think about the pain may make a person appear to be dealing with it well; but denial will only hide the pain, not erase it. Like the tide, the waves of grief may go out for a time, but they will go on lapping at the person's heels for years to come. At times, these waves will surge back in with great force, and often without warning. If a person doesn't eventually deal with these feelings, the feelings will eventually deal with the person.

Each particular kind of loss carries with it its own unique set of feelings and stages of adjustment. The death of any significant person will bring about a predictable series of emotions; however, depending on the specific circumstances, each death will also evoke a unique set of reactions characteristic of the situation itself. Some losses, for example, may be the result of an illness, either sudden or long-term. In such cases, family members may blame the healthcare system, holding it accountable for failing to save, or to find a timely cure for, their loved one. They may even direct their anger at the victim for not having taken better care of himself or herself. The pain and the anger behind it are an expected and perfectly natural reaction to having someone so important taken away.

We're bound to get angry whenever something of great value is taken away from us, especially if we feel the loss could or should have been prevented in the first place. This anger will strike whatever target it can safely find as it seeks to settle the score with whoever is responsible. Once released, the anger will subside and leave behind only a deep well of hurt in its wake.

We expect varying degrees of denial, anger, and blame to follow any significant loss; but, depending on the circumstances, loved ones may feel other feelings like guilt, remorse, regret, or even responsibility as well. In accidental deaths, family members may become angry with the circumstances surrounding the accident or perhaps even at the victim for not being more careful. But in all such cases, it is common for loved ones to try to reconstruct in their minds all of the events that led up to the tragedy. They will agonize over every detail in a desperate attempt to discover how it could have happened or to find out what they could have done to prevent it. Or they will dwell on how different things might have been had only a single detail of the situation been changed.

In deaths resulting from suicide, family members may have an understandably hard time swallowing the truth. They'll often search for any other explanation for the death than to believe that someone they love could have taken his or her own life. Or they will search in retrospect for the subtle warning signs they feel they missed. They may blame themselves for everything, holding themselves personally liable for not having seen these signs and stopped the tragedy from happening. They look in vain for answers, trying to comprehend what depth of despair could have driven someone to such desperation. Over and over in their minds they will play that tape of their last argument or conversation with the person they've lost. They wonder if perhaps they had just been too busy to have heard when the person called out for help. All of these prove to be futile attempts to find the clue that could have rerouted the tragic course of events.

And lastly, our increasingly dangerous society is making families all too familiar with the tragic reality of losing loved ones to violent crime. Occurrences of drive-by shootings, random assaults, carjackings, armed robberies, and homicidal shooting sprees are all too common as headline stories. But behind each and every headline is a family and a circle of friends left to cope with the sudden and senseless shattering of their worlds. Each event is equally tragic and carries with it a wide and complex range of emotions—from outrage at injustice to the overpowering force of revenge and the urge to strike back in return. The tragedy itself is surpassed only by each survivor's personal and private struggle to make sense out of what is truly senseless. But perhaps the most cruel aspect of these sudden and violent losses is that the loved ones are robbed of any opportunity to make peace with the person, to make amends where appropriate, and ultimately to say good-bye. Without this closure, such events can be difficult to release and nearly impossible to accept.

For those left behind in the wake of any such tragedy, the road to acceptance is a long and rocky one. Of course we all know that acceptance is the desired end result and final stage of a journey we know as the grieving process. But although it requires that we make peace with our loss, acceptance in no way implies that we make peace with the way the person died. Families who find themselves caught in the aftermath of tragic accidents or violent crimes have a real battle with the concept of *"acceptance"* because the word itself implies that they should *"accept"* what is quite simply unacceptable. But acceptance doesn't immediately translate into forgiveness, because there are some acts of inhumanity that are in their cruelty simply unforgivable. Acceptance and forgiveness are two very separate and individualized processes. To accept, we need only let go of the pain and move on, but to forgive, we must find some meaning in even the most meaningless of events.

At its most basic level, acceptance of the death of a loved one means that the wound is at last allowed to heal. The survivors are then able to pull their circle of loved ones together and at last close the gap left behind by the person's death.

With acceptance comes the realization that no one could ever fill the gap by stepping into the space, nor can any amount of distraction or denial effectively divert attention from the void on a permanent basis. True acceptance requires the acknowledgment that a piece of our lives is missing, and it allows healing in the spirit that the face of the family and the lives of those left behind have been forever and irreversibly changed.

Major losses are unfair, but that doesn't make them any less a fact of life. And the unfairness of it all doesn't make us any less responsible for finding the reasons and courage to carry on. Moving on with our lives is not a betrayal of the person who has died. Some believe that carrying on in the absence of loved ones suggests that they've been forgotten. Acceptance doesn't mean that we act as if the deceased were never here, or that they aren't important enough to hold us back from moving on—it merely gives us permission to continue on our life's journey without guilt or regret. We cannot and should not stop living our own lives because someone we love has been robbed of theirs. Nor should we deprive ourselves of the joy and fulfillment life has to offer simply to punish ourselves for being able to do so or to protest the injustice of it all.

If we are to fully appreciate the necessity of living through the pain in order to arrive at true acceptance, we have to bid farewell to a widely accepted but misleading cliché. In the face of tragedy and loss, we find ourselves seeking comfort in believing that, *"Time heals all wounds,"* when in reality, this expression couldn't be less true. Contrary to longstanding belief, there is nothing magical about time. Time itself has no healing powers and does nothing more for us than lessen the intensity of our pain by moving us farther away from the event that caused it. Only when coupled with openness, willingness, and a rugged desire to face the pain head-on does time afford us the opportunity to heal any wound.

If time itself did indeed heal all wounds, then everyone who has experienced a significant loss would at some point arrive automatically at a place of peaceful acceptance. Feelings of bitterness, hurt, and anger over our losses would expire when they exceeded their time limit. Although this sounds good in theory, it doesn't explain why some people struggle with the sharp pain of loss even years after a death, while others go on to find peace and eventual relief from their pain. Does our beloved time play favorites? Or maybe it's us, and not time, who decide the end result. Acceptance isn't random––assigned to some and not to others—it's something we earn. It's not a given, it's a possibility. And it's only a possibility for those who want it badly enough and have the courage to walk through the pain to get it.

But isn't there an easier way out? Like human nature in general, our emotions will try to seek out the path of least resistance. In other words, even our feelings will find an easier, softer way if there is one to be found. In this case, the easier, softer way is called *denial*. Denial is the easiest way out of pain because it provides us with immediate relief. Denial can also help us by buying time and preventing us from being overwhelmed by too many overpowering feelings before we're ready to deal with them. Denial can become very comfortable though, because like an anesthetic, it blocks the pain. But at some point it wears off and we're forced to venture out to face the pain.

Covering and concealing the hurt leads to wounds that are never allowed to fully heal. Do you really want a wound that aches for a lifetime to be the legacy of a loved one? It seems a more fitting tribute for you to celebrate the person's contribution to and enrichment of your life and focus on making the best of your own. The loss itself is tragic enough. For you to stop living a fulfilling life because of it would only double the tragedy, for then two lives would be lost instead of one.

Mattie

Mattie had a bitter pill to swallow. She had lost her only son, Jordan, at the tender age of 20 to a drive-by shooting, only to discover that he had a 6-month-old daughter by his ex-girlfriend. She found this out the night the girl's parents brought the baby to her door.

It was the day after the funeral. Their daughter had run away again and they just couldn't afford to take care of another baby. They already had too many mouths to feed. What could Mattie say?

"The nerve!" Mattie's brother said. "How dare they do that to you? They're taking advantage of you when your son's just died!" Despite her brother's outrage, Mattie felt that she'd somehow been given back a small piece of her son.

And when they caught the youth who had pulled the trigger, her brother was incensed. "I hope someone takes care of him in prison," he said. "He'll get what's coming to him someday." Her brother was shocked when Mattie told him that she wouldn't be poisoned by revenge. "I won't let him kill me, too," she said.

Mattie had a way of finding some glimmer of hope when no one else could see it. Of course she felt the pain. Of course she felt angry. There were even times when the pain of burying her only son was so intense that she wondered what she had done to deserve it. But when she felt this way, she reminded herself that her son was the one who lost his life, not her. She knew she couldn't have brought this tragedy upon herself because of something she had done. She knew she wasn't that powerful. So she celebrated her son's life and was grateful for the time she was given with him. She believed that her son would have been disappointed in her if she allowed his death to break her spirit.

At the sentencing, Mattie made a statement. She didn't have bitter or hateful words for the murderer; instead, she gave him a gift...her forgiveness. Mattie believed that doing this made her the winner in a losing situation.

She told him that she refused to let what he had done turn her into the kind of person he was. She had no room in her heart for hatred, and she pitied him because he did. She did this for her son. She did it for herself. She would never have forgiven herself if she hadn't. She believed that the murderer had been taken over by hatred and revenge and that her son had fallen victim to them. She wasn't about to let them have her, too. She was stronger than that.

Making Sense of Confusion: When a Parent Abuses Substances

Perhaps the most widespread problem in today's society that prevents parents from being able to care for their children is the rising tide of substance abuse. The disease of addiction takes complete control over every aspect of a person's life, and its effects spill over onto everyone with close ties to the addict. Although it isn't fully understood why some people will become dependent on alcohol and drugs while others do not, it is a fact that the desire to experiment with mind- and mood-altering substances is very much a part of our human experience.

The use and abuse of chemicals has been around nearly as long as humankind. It seems that ever since we've been aware of our own consciousness, we've been looking for ways to alter it. So if we resign ourselves to the fact that for as far back as we can recall, people have been in hot pursuit of whatever substance they could cultivate, dig up, ferment, harvest, smoke, snort, inject, ingest, digest, or inhale to alter the way they feel, we can safely say that the centuries-old practice of getting high is in no danger of going anywhere soon.

As science and technology make great leaps forward, there will always be those who'll find ways to channel this progress into the development of new and more effective ways of addicting our population. Each new and more potent mixture we concoct is added to our existing arsenal of addictive substances, making chemical abuse increasingly more common and frighteningly more dangerous. Today, it's nearly impossible to find anyone whose life has not been touched in some way by someone's abuse of chemicals.

It would be overly simplistic to say that thoroughly understanding the disease of addiction on its own will make the problem easier to deal with, but not having that understanding will make it even more difficult. It's certainly possible for us to fight an enemy that we don't understand, but then the only weapon we have to use against it is brute force. The more we know about our enemies, the better equipped we are to strategize ways of outwitting them. Likewise, if we don't understand addiction, we're likely to make the mistake of trying to overpower it by using brute force. With addiction, our best defense is not so much to conquer it outright, but rather to outsmart it.

The most important thing you'll need to learn if you have someone in your life who is caught in the grasp of addiction is the fine art of separating the person from the disease. If you have an addicted person in your life, you've probably felt all kinds of confusing and contradictory emotions. You've probably felt both rage and pity at the same time, just as you've probably felt hurt and sympathy, betrayal and concern, helplessness, inadequacy, hope, fear, indignation, guilt, mercy, and remorse all rolled up into one. In sorting through this mess, it's a great help for you to be able to identify which of these feelings you feel toward the *person* and which ones you feel toward the *problem*. In other words, you may *love* your children, but you may *hate* what they're doing to themselves.

Making this separation requires that you be able to distinguish the person from the behavior. If you can't make this distinction, you're likely to see the person as the problem instead of the addiction, and you're likely to make the person the enemy. This can make an antagonistic and adversarial relationship out of one that's tense to begin with.

Keep in mind that you love someone who has a problem called addiction. It's entirely possible, and quite probable, that you're capable of loving someone while despising their behavior or lifestyle. You're always on the same team when it comes to people you love, even if you're in bitter disagreement about what they're doing. As teammates, you share a mutual opponent called addiction. Addiction is the villain here. It's responsible for destroying the life of a person you care about, and it's the thing that's tearing your family apart. When you separate the person from the problem, you focus on the problem, not the person. We deal much more objectively and effectively with problems than we do with people. The emotions we feel toward the person can distort our ability to see the problem clearly.

Because of the kinds of behaviors involved and the kinds of feelings these behaviors bring up in people, it's hard for many to see addiction as an illness, but it is. It's not *willful misconduct* and insisting that it is only makes us angrier and more judgmental of the addict. An addicted person is a sick person in need of treatment, not a bad person in need of punishment. No illness has ever been cured by rage or scorn. Would you reasonably expect to cure a diabetic by becoming angry with that person? *"But,"* you might say, *"these diseases are different. The diabetic couldn't help it. Addicts and alcoholics shouldn't get any sympathy, because they brought this on themselves."*

Certainly each person who becomes addicted has at some point made a conscious decision to experiment with a drug of choice, but haven't we all played with fire? Experimentation with alcohol and drugs is a choice made by countless hundreds of thousands of people every day without consequence. Why don't they get hooked? Are some people weaker than others? Certainly, the use of alcohol and drugs is a choice, but becoming addicted is not.

Not everyone who experiments with substances falls into the trap of addiction. And those who do aren't weak in character, they're just more vulnerable to the lure of the drug. This vulnerability is not a character defect or a moral weakness, and it shouldn't be treated as one. Look at it this way if you will—getting addicted is a *possible* consequence of drug and alcohol use just as lung cancer is a possible consequence of smoking. Not all smokers develop lung cancer, and not all of those who use alcohol or drugs will become addicted. What makes people more vulnerable in both cases? Now, there is the million dollar question! Can we predict which smokers will develop lung cancer and which will not? Not any more effectively than we can predict which alcohol and drug users will become dependent.

Perhaps the most important concept to understand with regard to chemical dependency is that, no matter what caused the problem, it needs treatment just the same. Condemning lung cancer patients for smoking in the first place doesn't rid them of their cancer. Does the medical field give preferential treatment to lung cancer patients who didn't smoke? Are we more empathic when patients don't bring the disease on themselves? No. Once the cancer is there, it doesn't matter what caused it; it requires standard treatment just the same. Being angry with a person for doing risky things may be an understandable human response to what seems like irrational behavior, but it doesn't change the fact that the person still needs help. Being angry at the addict for playing Russian roulette with drugs doesn't treat the addiction.

If we persist in the belief that addiction is a choice our loved ones have made consciously and knowingly, then we're more inclined to get angry with them for the things the addiction makes them do. When we lose our objectivity about the nature of the problem, we get caught up in the mindset of, *"If he had any respect at all for me, he wouldn't drink so much,"* or even believe that, *"If she loved her child so much, she wouldn't use drugs."*

Don't lose perspective and begin to feel that the addict's behavior is directed at you personally. The alcoholic isn't drinking *at* you, and the addict isn't using *at* you; they're doing it to themselves while you stand by as a compassionate witness to their self-destructive behavior. If you feel this behavior is personal, you're guaranteed to feel angry and betrayed by the treatment (or mistreatment, as the case may be) they're inflicting on you.

You and your family certainly do suffer as a result, but, when you think about it, not nearly as much as the addict. This is not to say that it's a family's duty to sit idly by and silently suffer the consequences in the name of compassion, but it is to say that taking it personally will only deepen the injury and intensify the pain you're already feeling.

Family members must also be careful not to get caught up in the pointless game of feeling responsible for the person's addiction. If you believe it's your fault, you'll think it's your responsibility to cure the disease. Parents in particular often allow themselves to be wracked with guilt, wondering what they could have possibly done to have driven their children to drugs.

I assure you that whatever you may or may not have done, it's not your fault. You don't have the power to make someone drink or use drugs any more than you have the power to make them stop. Never take responsibility for someone's addiction––if you do, you'll lay yourself wide open to be fiercely manipulated by your own guilt. And *never* insert yourself between a person and his or her addiction in an attempt to control or stop it—this is an extremely unrewarding place to be and will leave you emotionally flattened, as if you'd been struck by an oncoming train. Addiction is just as powerful. If the addict can't control it, you certainly can't.

You can best help yourself and drug- or alcohol-dependent loved ones by allowing them to struggle with their own disease process and lovingly letting them bear the brunt of whatever consequences and crises go along with it. Don't get into the ring with them. Stay on the sidelines with care and compassion, but don't get in the middle. And *never* make yourself the clean-up crew after the fight. Taking responsibility for their behavior or protecting them from the consequences of it is called *enabling* because it enables them to continue doing it. Enabling behaviors deprive them of the opportunity to see that what they're doing is causing problems for everyone.

In rescuing, protecting, defending, minimizing, and making excuses for their unhealthy and self-destructive behavior, your good intentions and sincere desire to help those who abuse alcohol or drugs will only backfire in the end. These behaviors erase the evidence and reinforce their delusion that their drinking or using really isn't a problem. People are most compelled to change when they're in enough pain or when their old patterns of behavior stop working for them. No one is inspired to fix what doesn't appear to be broken, and they certainly won't be inspired to fix it if you keep fixing it for them.

Amanda

Amanda retired at 62 from her life-long career as a school teacher. She had dreamt of moving in with her sister in Las Vegas so the two of them could squander their retirement money together playing the slot machines and traveling the globe. Now at 70, her life couldn't be further from that dream. She'd spent her first eight years of retirement battling with Brian, her 40-year-old, cocaine-addicted son. Brian had three children by three different women. Amanda had inherited Lily, the youngest of the three. She had taken Lily in when Brian went into his first treatment program. At that time Lily was 4 years old.

Lily is now 11 and has stayed with Amanda through the many times Brian has been in and out of the house. She wouldn't dream of having Lily stay anywhere else, but since retiring, her life has been an endless blur of lies, excuses, and broken promises.

Brian had been fired from every job and had lost every apartment he'd managed to get for the better part of the past four years. And every time, Amanda had taken him back in.

He'd been in more treatment programs than she's had hot breakfasts because she diligently made sure his private medical insurance was paid for out of the money she had set aside.

She's paid his traffic tickets, bailed him out of jail, accepted his collect calls in the middle of the night, advanced him money he promised he'd pay back the minute he got back on his feet, paid his rent, made excuses to his many bosses about why he hadn't made it to work again, and sat up more nights than she could recall looking at the clock and worrying that she'd never hear his key in the door again.

Brian, on the other hand, thought all of his Christmases had come at once. He stole her TV, cashed her pension checks, "loaned" her car to the drug dealer to keep from having his kneecaps broken, pawned the watch her mother had specially inscribed for her, bullied her, lied to her, blamed her, intimidated her, threatened to take his daughter away if she stopped supporting him, and promised her until he was blue in the face that he would change if she just gave him "one more chance."

The night he came home looking crazed, babbling about the house being bugged by the CIA, he had gone too far.

He demanded Lily give him the little allowance money she had carefully tucked away in her shoebox—and he wasn't joking. The fear in Lily's eyes tore like a knife through Amanda's heart. He wasn't the man they both knew anymore. There was a coldness in his eyes. He was scaring them, and Amanda believed that the man who had come home that night was fully prepared to kill them both over $7.76. Amanda had had enough.

The next day she found herself sitting in a counselor's office in the very same program Brian had been in so many times himself. She wanted to know why the program hadn't helped him. They needed to lock him up before he hurt someone.

Amanda wasn't prepared for the counselor to tell her that she was part of the problem. And she certainly wasn't prepared to hear that they couldn't do anything for Brian until he was ready to help himself—but they had plenty of help for her.

It was the reality check she'd needed, and it was the beginning of a new chapter in Amanda's life. She had gone to the center to get help for Brian and ended up finding a new voice for herself.

She began to understand that giving Brian false ultimatums showed him that there were no real consequences for him. And she learned that she needed to stop believing what he said he was going to do and instead, start believing what he actually did. She also learned that she didn't have to throw him out into the street to show she meant what she said.

She decided instead to give Brian the option to stay at home— this time under the condition that he got back into treatment and gave her permission to monitor his progress.

Slowly, things began to change. But they couldn't change until Amanda decided that she wanted to be a part of Brian's life more than she wanted to be a part of his self-destruction. It was difficult, and it took courage for her to begin standing up to him after all those years. But in her eyes she had nothing to lose.

There was a time not so long ago when Amanda was afraid her son would die if she stopped taking care of him...until she came to the realization that the way they were living was killing them both.

Disappointment and Betrayal: When a Parent is Unreliable

Addiction is only one reason why a parent may not be able to rise to the duty of adequately caring for a child. Many grandparents take over the primary care of their grandchildren when the parents are too young, when they are emotionally or mentally unable to handle the strain, or are simply unable to make sound judgments on a child's behalf—whether distracted by their own problems or preoccupied by other pursuits.

For example, a parent in an abusive relationship or one who has turned to illegal activities like dealing drugs, stealing, or prostitution to manage mounting debts lives in a world that is unsafe for a child. Such parents have enough trouble worrying about their own survival and will often be relieved if offered the opportunity to relinquish the child to another's care. Other parents are too preoccupied with their own careers, educations, or personal pursuits to spare enough time to care for a child. In such cases, the grandparents offer the child the time and attention the parent is unable or unwilling to sacrifice.

As with the chemically dependent parent, having an unreliable parent exposes a child to a never-ending series of hurts. These deep emotional wounds cannot heal, because they're constantly being reopened. In this respect, an unpredictable or unreliable parent can be even more damaging to a child than an absent one. Although the tragedy of total loss can't be emphasized enough, the death of a parent is a hurt that is finite and irreversible—a pain that comes in one overwhelming blow. The adjustment is dramatic and ongoing, but the blow itself is swift and final. On the other hand, the pain of having a parent who can't be counted on comes in many smaller but more continuous blows. The injuries are ongoing, leaving a child barely able to recover before the next one comes.

The unpredictable or unreliable parent poses an ongoing series of dilemmas for both the children and the grandparents. The position of the grandparents as surrogate parents is unsteady and subject to the changing whims of the child's true parents. Grandparents in these situations are left feeling helpless and powerless, with no real clout or leverage to use to their advantage. Afraid of making waves and possibly losing the grandchildren altogether, the grandparents are forced to bow to the demands of the parent, however irrational or unpredictable they may be.

Although the grandparents may be much better judges of what is in the best interest of the children, our powerful legal system doesn't pay much heed to their opinions. The reality is that if either biological parent is anywhere in the picture, no one (not even another well-meaning and devoted family member) outranks them in the eyes of the law where their children are concerned.

Only in extreme cases, such as those in which a child is being severely neglected or abused, will another party have any legal authority to come between parent and child. For the vast number of grandparents, the responsibility of raising their grandchildren has been taken on in a *Good Samaritan* spirit, by choice rather than a result of legal intervention. When it comes time to fight for legal rights, grandparents more likely than not are left with strong convictions but no one who'll listen to them.

With an unreliable parent in the picture, the grandparents' role in the lives of their grandchildren is always subject to change without notice. In an attempt to gain some control or sense of security with regard to their grandchildren's welfare, some grandparents explore the possibility of adoption. But if one or both biological parents are still around, adoption is really not an option for grandparents. Even in cases in which the parents might be willing to sign away parental rights, many grandparents still opt not to pursue legal routes like adoption because the children are already part of the family. The irony is that, in spite of the fact that they are blood relatives, grandparents raising their grandchildren have less real legal say in the lives of their grandchildren than do foster or adoptive parents.

The real absurdity here is that, because adoption and foster parenting are formal arrangements recognized by legal authorities, they are subject to monitoring, set standards, and strict regulations that blood relatives are not. Adoptive and foster parents must apply and be approved before being granted this status, whereas in real family situations, no such application or approval process exists. Natural or biological families (unfortunately) have no such built-in protection. The fact of the matter is that grandparents who take in their grandchildren are, in most cases, providing an act of good faith and nothing more in the eyes of the law. This sets the stage for these children to become entangled in a custodial tug-of-war in which the parents are able to drop the children off with the grandparents at their convenience and for whatever length of time they choose, only to return for them whenever the mood strikes. Even if the grandparents' home is more fit and provides a more stable environment for the children, there may be moral and ethical grounds but no legal grounds for the grandparents to refuse to return the children whenever the parents demand it.

Being caught in a tug-of-war between a child and an unpredictable or unreliable parent is truly an undesirable place to be. This makes the task of keeping the conflicts that arise be-

tween parent and grandparent away from the children a difficult one. It would be unrealistic to expect that grandparents
could play a convincing game of make-believe for their grandchildren, creating an illusion that there are no problems in this
area. Logically speaking, if the children are not permanently
with their parents, this is in itself evidence to the children that
there is a problem somewhere. No grandparent could realistically be expected to pull off the illusion of a perfect family if
this in fact is not the case.

One of the challenges facing grandparents who have an unstable parent on their hands is striking a balance between
telling the child *too little* and telling the child *too much*. As with
anything, either extreme is unhealthy and carries with it its
own set of problems. Unfortunately, there is no standard way
for grandparents to determine how little is too little and how
much is too much. Each situation is different, and each child is
unique, not only in terms of age but also personality, maturity,
and level of understanding. In some respects, these variables
make it easier, while at the same time making it more complicated, for grandparents to decide just how much detail to
disclose.

In making this decision, don't forget that children are just
that—children. Although they may not be completely shut off
to what's going on around them, they're also not miniature
adults with the mental sophistication to piece together the big
picture of what's going on in their world. As a rule, children
know much more than we think they do, but they understand
much less than we expect them to.

In general, children have a tremendous ability to sense the
mood and feelings around them. They're skilled at taking the
emotional temperature of their environment and are acutely
aware when things are not quite right. They may not have developed the ability to reason out the situation and understand
exactly what's wrong, but it is extremely likely that in a
mixed-up environment, they know that *something* is wrong—
they just won't be able to pinpoint exactly what it is.

To broaden our understanding of how children perceive
their world, let's take a moment to step into the mind of a
young boy. His world is very small. His universe is typically

only as large as his immediate surroundings. All that exists for him is what he is able to see or touch or experience at the moment. Until the age of about 5 to 7, he doesn't have the ability to *"abstract."* In other words, he hasn't developed the ability to understand that things happen outside his perception. Until he develops this skill, anything that takes place beyond his immediate perception doesn't exist. For example, when a parent leaves the room or drops a child off at day care, the child will cry uncontrollably because of his inability to understand that an object that leaves his sight still exists. When an object (in this case, the parent) is no longer visible, in this child's mind, the parent has disappeared altogether. This is what makes the game of "peek-a-boo" so much more interesting to children than it is to adults! Until a child develops the ability to abstract, his world is a place full of surprises.

This limited perspective places each child at the center of his or her own universe. Given too little information, children who sense trouble are likely to conclude that the problems have something to do with them. This is why so many children who have never been told they're to blame for the family's problems will draw this very conclusion all on their own. Even as adults, it can be hard for us to shake these long-standing beliefs. We go on through life feeling we were really responsible for our parents' divorce or believing that we caused our parents to abuse, neglect, or reject us. The beliefs that are branded on us in childhood die hard. Unless we were given the proper support and guidance, we can miss that important developmental stage where we learn that our world is bigger than we thought. If we never got the chance to set the record straight, a childhood stage of development can turn into a life-long feeling of responsibility for something we didn't do.

If you assume that children aren't able to sense that there are problems around them, you won't feel the need to discuss those problems with them. This gives them too much room to put the pieces of information together in a way that puts them at fault. We have to avoid making the mistake of assuming that if children aren't able to fully understand what the problem is, they won't notice that one exists. With too little information, children who sense trouble are likely to conclude that it's of their own doing.

If, for these children, nothing existed before they came along and nothing exists that doesn't directly involve them, they won't be able to understand that their parents' problems began long before they arrived on the scene. With only their own limited reasoning to go on, they are in essence trying to complete a jigsaw puzzle without a master picture to guide them. The best they can do on their own is to assemble the loose pieces in a way that makes sense to them but that may in reality bear little resemblance to the real and complete picture.

The trick here lies in giving children enough information to confirm their feelings and perceptions without overwhelming them with too much detail. If there are problems and you act as if there are none, children become confused and anxious because they're being told that what they're feeling isn't real. It's best in these instances to acknowledge that problems do exist while making certain to reassure them that they are not the cause. The details about the exact nature and cause of the trouble are less important in children's minds than the confirmation that what they're feeling is indeed on target. Until they develop the mental ability to digest the big picture, children's concerns are really quite simple. All they really want to know are the answers to three basic questions:

1. *"What's going on?"*
2. *"Is it my fault?"*
3. *"Is someone dealing with it?"*

Given this, when times are tough, you can significantly reduce a child's anxiety by consistently reinforcing these three basic messages:

1. *Problems do indeed exist.*
2. *The child is not the cause.*
3. *Someone trustworthy is in control of the situation.*

Leaving any of these three basic questions unanswered leaves too much room for a child to feel unnecessarily anxious or fearful. All three messages are equally important, and none should be taken for granted by assuming the child already knows the answer.

"But aren't we supposed to protect children from life's problems at all cost?" you might well wonder.

"Absolutely not!" I would reply—because knowing that problems exist and that they're being dealt with is significantly different from knowing that problems exist and not being sure if anyone is in control. Knowing about problems is not nearly as traumatic for children as the feeling that there isn't anyone they can trust to handle them. Difficulties alone won't threaten a child's sense of safety or security—it can be threatened only by a child's fear that there is no one stronger and wiser to trust these difficulties to.

At the opposite end of the spectrum from keeping a child in the dark with regard to a parent's problems, lies giving a child too much information.

The tendency to over-involve a child in the details of the family's problems occurs most often in homes where the parent/grandparent is isolated and lacks social and emotional support from other adults. A child in these situations can come to serve as a friend or confidant to the parent figure who is in desperate need of a sympathetic ear or a shoulder to cry on. Talking openly and freely with a child is never discouraged, and it would be impossible to completely protect a child from the emotional upheaval the grandparent is feeling. But it's wise to remember that, although you may be comforting allies to each other, you are not friends.

Allowing children unrestricted access to your day-to-day stresses can leave them either overwhelmed and confused or feeling as though they should try to do something to help.

After an episode of blowing off steam, a grandparent may walk away feeling relieved, while the child is left feeling thunderstruck. Such exchanges might ease the burdens of the grandparent, but they add to the burdens of the child. A child's shoulders by nature are smaller and weaker than an adult's, so we must provide only as much information as a child can comfortably handle, delivered in bite-sized pieces.

Parent figures who discuss the gory details of financial pressures and personal or family conflicts can unknowingly cause children to worry over things they're not yet able to comprehend and certainly have no power to change. Instead of understanding that blowing off steam is a necessary release of pressure, children take it as a sign that their grandparents can't cope and may be losing control. When adults are busily relieving stress by unloading it, children are often busily taking it on as their own.

It's the adult's job to find healthy ways of handling life's pressures, to let the children in on only what is necessary, and to protect them from the rest. It's the job of the child to benefit from this, free from worries and able to enjoy just being a child. Again, it's perfectly okay for a child to know that the ship has sprung a leak, but if the only one the child trusts to plug it up seems to be losing control, they're both sunk.

In addition to managing the many pressures of parenting someone else's child, your challenges are further increased by the fact that you are caught in the middle between a child and an unpredictable or unreliable parent. In many cases, the competition between you and the parent for the child's affection, the child's loyalty, and the right to have the final say in matters concerning the child can be heated and even downright ugly. It's truly an art for any grandparent dealing with an unstable parent to keep disagreements with the parent from clouding the grandparent-grandchild relationship. By keeping these feelings and issues separated, you remove your grandchild from the firing line and prevent him or her from becoming an unintended target of any anger that was intended for the parent.

Many grandparents and grandchildren live in a perpetual state of disappointment when there is an unstable parent afoot. They eagerly await the time when the parent will make a dramatic turnaround and suddenly take on the parental role with the seriousness and heartfelt commitment it deserves. If your grandchild is in your care because the parent has proven to be irresponsible for any number of reasons, you would be wise to keep realistic expectations of such a parent.

With a chemically dependent parent, for example, the kinds of disappointments you can expect will take the form of those heartbreaking waits for the parent to arrive for a long-anticipated visit, or promises made only later to be broken, or even the heartache of enduring long and painful periods with no contact at all while birthdays and holidays pass unacknowledged.

With parents who are either too young or unwilling to face the obligations of parenthood, similar disappointments may be in store. They may include the child's painful realization that he or she ranks second in the parent's life to the pursuit of relationships or the allure of an exciting social life that takes precedence over a child's life. Such disappointments are painful in their own right, but they can be deepened if both grandparent and grandchild hold out the unrealistic hope that, *"It'll be different this time."*

At the risk of sounding like a defeatist—irresponsible behavior breeds irresponsible behavior. Having a child (or several, for that matter) will not instantly turn a reckless person into a model of responsibility. Nor can simply having a child be expected to widen a self-centered individual's narrow focus to make room for another person.

Becoming a parent in itself is not promised to be a character building experience for anyone; in fact, for some, the added strain of parenthood wears down what little strength of character they may have had to begin with. Although there are cases in which irresponsible people are able to rise brilliantly to the challenge of parenthood, it's probably safe to assume that if this had been the case with your child, your grandchildren wouldn't be with you now.

Impulsive, irresponsible, and self-centered lifestyles are precisely the reason why so many children need to be placed in the care of others. Responsible people for the most part are less likely to have children they're unprepared to care for. Careless disregard for the consequences of their impulsive behavior doesn't start when people become parents—it was in place long before they gave life to a child. If these behaviors were in place and were ultimately responsible for them having children in the first place, it may be a sad but logical assumption that these behaviors will follow them into parenthood. You shouldn't be surprised when an irresponsible and self-centered person becomes an irresponsible and self-centered parent who is ill-equipped and unprepared to make the necessary sacrifices to care properly for a child.

If a parent is chemically dependent, don't let it surprise you if that person behaves in an irrational, impulsive, and unpredictable manner. This is what addicted people do. If these adjectives describe your addicted child to a tee, it doesn't mean your child is a bad person, it means she or he is simply acting the way addicted people act, parent or not. Addiction can suddenly turn the most stable and reliable people into people who are untrustworthy and out of control—that is just the nature of the disease. Until addicts find recovery, it's self-defeating to expect them to behave in any manner other than that which is characteristic of addicted individuals.

If your child's failure to look before leaping is the main reason you now have a grandchild to care for, you may be annoyed, but you shouldn't be surprised if that adult child falls short of taking complete responsibility for being a parent. It's a true sign of maturity when individuals are willing to accept the consequences of their actions, regardless of whether the results were expected or unexpected, desired or not. And it's this very lack of maturity and unwillingness to accept the consequences of personal actions that becomes the breeding ground for so many parentless children. A mature person does what he or she *has* to do; an immature person does only what he or she *wants* to do.

Rather than becoming angry with your children because of their shortsightedness, you'll find more peace if you learn to accept these shortcomings as part of the complex package that makes up the individuals they are. Many grandparents feel that letting go of their anger at the inadequate parent means they're indirectly giving their seal of approval to that parent's unacceptable behavior. Acceptance in this regard is entirely for your benefit and yours alone. It has more to do with how you've chosen to make sense of the situation than with the acceptability or unacceptability of the situation itself. Accepting a situation we don't have the power to change makes us stronger and more able to cope, because it stops us from wasting our time and energy being angry, frustrated, and disappointed when people or situations are being exactly the way they're supposed to be.

By the above, I don't mean to imply that the only way to achieve peace of mind with a difficult person in our lives is to tolerate the intolerable and call it acceptance. In determining how much we're willing to tolerate, we mustn't forget our moral obligation to always be willing to stand up for what we believe in and to speak out against what we believe to be unjust, unfair, or morally corrupt. But in so doing, we owe it to ourselves to understand that the only person whose behavior we not only have the *power* to change but the *right* to change is ourselves. Like it or not, there will always be injustice in the world. And there will always be dishonesty, deceit, cruelty, and inhumanity somewhere, no matter how far we travel. And there is a reason for this, because without these ills, there would be no true acts of courage or heroism. Although we can make small and individual differences in what we each do personally, we still lack the power to make the insensitive person feel, the ignorant person understand, or the corrupt person reform. With this in mind, our task must then be to remain unwavering in our own convictions and to find a way of keeping the insanity around us from driving us insane.

It is troublesome enough that there are individuals among us who lack the capacity to fully comprehend the impact their words and deeds have on others. We only add to this tragedy by making their troubles our own. Chaos in the world around us is a given...we can't stop it. But allowing the insanity that surrounds us to make us lose sight of our goals, our direction, or our convictions is a tragedy we can prevent. Allowing a troubled person with a lousy attitude to disturb our peace is not only foolhardy but also unnecessary. By refusing to allow these individuals to upset us, we avoid being drawn into their world of negativity and distorted logic. When we don't play the game, we put their problems back in their own laps instead of leaving them in ours. This concept is essential here because for many of us, these troubled individuals come not only in the form of random strangers, but as members of our own families.

The irony for most grandparents, as it may be for you, is that, while you are at home busily working on an ulcer over what your adult children may or may not be doing, they aren't feeling even a fraction of the stress you're feeling. They're out there doing exactly as they please and giving you ulcers at the same time! See how powerful you've allowed your children to become in your life—so powerful that they can drive you to utter distraction simply by being themselves...and they have the power to give you an ulcer without even having to give it a moment's thought! You've been drawn into their insanity and are now being held hostage by your fantasy that they'll suddenly change their ways. This is not to say that you should give up on them. Change is always possible, but it's a good bet that many of these adult children will have trouble seeing the need for change because they're doing exactly what they want to do—it's you, on the other hand, who's suffering. *Now* who seems to have the problem?

With these kinds of people and situations, our best revenge is to regain control over our own lives and to stop allowing someone else's actions to control our emotions. Arriving at a place of peace in this regard doesn't mean that we accept what the individual is doing as being healthy or even morally right; it simply gives us back our energy so that we can put it to better use in impacting what small part of the situation we have the ability to change.

We can't force our children to be good parents, but we can stop punishing them for their shortcomings, stop making excuses for their unhealthy behavior, and stop expecting them to see things the way we do. Your greatest power lies not in changing the parents, but in protecting their children from instability by making sure they get the safety and stability their parents can't provide.

Besides, who are we to say that anyone needs to change to suit us?

While we're busy taking stock of how another adult is living his or her life, we're placing ourselves in an authority position and claiming that we know what's ultimately best for that individual. All we can really know and judge is what's right for ourselves. When we're dissatisfied with what another person is doing, it's not just because we disagree with the action; it's usually because it's having a negative impact on us or reflecting negatively on us in some way. There are certainly healthy and unhealthy lifestyle choices, just as there are constructive and destructive ways of living. But each of us has the right to decide for ourselves which path we'll pursue; and most of us seem to have the same options available to us.

When we stand in judgment of the choices other people make, we're essentially saying that those individuals don't have the right to be who they are and to choose what they want for themselves. If we acknowledge that each of us is a separate person with an individual destiny, and that each of us has a path of our own making and a unique purpose, then who are we to say that anyone else needs to change at all? Another person's destiny is not up to us to choose—and we can't want more for others (not even family members we dearly love) than they want for themselves.

We show the greatest respect for others when we allow them to be human and flawed, as we are, and stop punishing them for it. We waste far too much energy being angry at others because they're not doing what we want them to do, or they're not choosing for themselves what we would have chosen for them. By backing up and out of their choices, we stand a better chance of giving them our opinions or advice and having our input received as a loving suggestion instead of judgment, nagging, or criticism. If we operate from such a place, we're able to show our loved ones that we care, but that we disagree with what they're doing. We're able to be there to offer another point of view, but we have enough respect for them to let them make their own mistakes and to learn from them. The implication that we know what's best for someone else will always be met with resistance, resentment, and careless disregard.

By learning to accept that things (and people as well) are not always as we would like them to be, we earn a sense of serenity that no one else has the power to take from us. No longer will the unwise or misguided actions of others have the power to disturb our inner peace. So while the lives of others may be in complete disarray, and while our circumstances may be just as trying and emotionally draining, we can still find some personal resolve in knowing that our happiness or unhappiness remains in our own hands. You can love and accept your children while steadfastly disagreeing with the way they live their lives. Master this skill. With an undependable parent, it's one your grandchildren will desperately need to learn.

Shayla

It may be a terrible thing to say, but Shayla's 8-year-old daughter is more mature than she is. At 24, Shayla is still behaving like the spoiled 15-year-old she was when she got pregnant. She fights with her mother about cleaning her room, she yells at her father because he's rude to her friends on the phone, and she runs the streets with her friends at all hours of the day and night. Her job at the mall is barely enough to make a dent in the parking tickets and credit card debts she's racked up. Worst of all, she treats her daughter, Phoebe, as if she were her younger sister. She is jealous of Phoebe and accuses her parents of doing more for Phoebe than they ever did for her.

Her parents are stuck. Because Shayla couldn't possibly take care of Phoebe on her own, they let them stay. If they put Shayla out, she says she'll take Phoebe with her. Her parents would take a much firmer approach with her...if only she didn't have a child.

And Phoebe worries about her mother. At eight, she's already started having adult-sized headaches and stomach problems. Shayla says she's just trying to get attention. She doesn't know that Phoebe sits up at night waiting for her to come home. Sometimes she doesn't. Sometimes she disappears for the whole day and Phoebe doesn't know when, or if, she's coming home. Phoebe is afraid her mother will forget about her one day and not come home anymore. Shayla doesn't know that Phoebe protects her, too. She isn't there when Phoebe pleads with her grandparents not to be mad at her mother and not to yell at her when she comes home.

Phoebe's grandparents are truly caught in the middle. They've tried everything. They've fought with Shayla, they've nagged Shayla, they've lectured Shayla, and they've used guilt on Shayla. They love Shayla... they just don't like her sometimes. They've done all of this for the sake of Phoebe.

When Phoebe's headaches and stomachaches started, they took her to a doctor. The doctor referred her to a child psychologist who charged them $75 to tell her grandparents one thing. "It's always been my experience," he said, "that if you fix the family, the child will get well."

The psychologist was right. The fighting had to stop. Phoebe's symptoms were telling them that the whole family was sick. They got into family counseling...without Shayla.

Over time, the grandparents came to the conclusion that Shayla was an adult who had a right to destroy her life if she so chose. It was their job to stop her from destroying Phoebe in the process. They came to accept that, like it or not, Shayla was who she was. Fighting with her wasn't going to make her into the kind of parent or even the kind of person they wanted her to be. They left her alone. They realized that Shayla's threat to leave and take Phoebe with her was just so much hot air. Having sole responsibility for Phoebe would have put too much of a crimp in her lifestyle.

Phoebe would probably be with them for good. So they set about giving her what Shayla could not. They stopped trying to force Shayla into a role she didn't want and began to teach Phoebe that even though Shayla loved her, there would always be things her mother just wouldn't be able to give her—and it wasn't her fault. Phoebe understood.

And the pain went away.

Inheriting a Troubled Child

Grandparents who are charged with raising their grand-children already have enough on their minds without adding to the mix the inevitable onslaught of endless childhood demands and the agony of adolescent acting out. Measured against the pressures of mounting bills, keeping a roof overhead, holding down a job, and now having more mouths to feed, any stress or pressure the grandchildren might feel seems to pale in comparison. Atop the day-to-day management of household responsibilities, having to deal with a child who is angry, rebellious, headstrong, defiant, or downright difficult to figure out just seems to add insult to injury.

But let us not forget that children who are taken in by their grandparents have begun their life's journey in a deficit situation. The odds are stacked against them from the start. Feeling abandoned and cast aside before they reach their grandparents' door, their defense systems are solidly in place at a very early age. Given that the legacy of physical and emotional abuse, loss, hurt, abandonment, neglect, chaos, fear, and confusion are all part of the baggage these children have securely packed for their journey to grandma's house, this chapter will serve as a road map for you in identifying and navigating the most common sources of miscommunication and misunderstanding between grandparents and grandchildren.

Here you'll gather what tools you'll need to maneuver around these roadblocks without losing your sanity along the way. Fasten your seatbelt...you're in for a bumpy ride!

Anger—Your Handiest Tool or Your Deadliest Weapon

For grandparents and grandchildren alike, anger is a familiar commodity. It's just a natural product of their individual circumstances. As sure as you can expect the grandparents to be angry at having to raise children that aren't their own, you can expect that these children will feel angry at having stand-ins where their parents ought to be. Anger, with all of the internal and external conflicts it creates, can prove to be one of the most destructive forces in such family relationships—that is, unless it's put in its proper perspective.

Any weapon can be turned into a tool with the right know-how. In reality, anger is a vital emotional messenger whose purpose is to alert us to the fact that something is amiss in our world. If we listen carefully to its message, we can gather important insight into the nature of life's problems and gain valuable information about what needs to be done to fix them. We ignore it at our own risk.

First and foremost in learning to crack the secret code of anger, understand that there are no "good" or "bad" feelings. All feelings are equally valuable. The only "good" and "bad" with regard to feelings is in how we react to them. We can't control what we *feel*, but we can control what we *do* in response. By labeling our feelings, we brand some of them "bad" and try not to feel them. The first step for anyone in learning to deal effectively with anger in particular is to strip it of its label of being "bad" which, in turn, gives us permission to feel it.

Feeling angry is not so much *bad*, as it is simply *human*. It's only human to become angry when we're hurt, afraid, or vulnerable, or when we're put in situations that make us feel helpless or taken advantage of. In these instances, we *should* feel angry. Grandparents who are raising their grandchildren are, after all, only human and are therefore subject to feel all of these things at one time or another. The problem isn't so much that we're angry, but that we're uncomfortable with the fact that we're angry and are not open to what it's telling us.

If anger is a natural consequence of many difficult life situations, then we can conclude that holding it back is unnatural and takes much more effort than expressing it freely. But by expressing anger too freely and in ineffective ways, we can create a whole new set of problems. Instead of fighting it, it's far better for us to develop a healthy respect for our anger, to learn to decipher its code, and to use its power to our advantage.

The internal tension that anger generates in each of us seeks natural release like steam inside a pressure valve. Each person is capable of retaining only so much internal pressure before the valve explodes. If this pressure isn't released gradually to maintain an even level, the tension builds steadily while the person fights to contain it. Living like this is hazardous because a fatigued valve is likely to blow haphazardly and often unexpectedly at the slightest increase in pressure.

It's no mystery why friends and neighbors of the person who has suddenly snapped, embarking on a murderous rampage will curiously describe this individual as someone *"nice,"* *"quiet,"* and who *"keeps to himself."* While this person has kept an even-tempered outward appearance, the internal pressure has been mounting, building steadily, until one day it reached its breaking point. There is a wise old adage that warns us to be wary of those who get angry at everything or at nothing. Those who appear to be bothered by nothing are either so incredibly well-adjusted that they should be avoided just because of their uncanny ability to make the rest of us look bad, or they're playing a dangerous game of make-believe.

Ironically, those who don't let out their anger don't get rid of it by burying it; they just hide it, forcing it to surface indirectly or in even more devious or destructive ways. For example, in families where parents are busy *"playing nice"* and pretending to live together in perfect harmony, their anger is often expressed in roundabout ways. While they think they're doing a convincing job of hiding their displeasure, it's often quite apparent to others—particularly to those sensitive and perceptive others we call children. Parents and grandparents alike who try to keep their angry feelings in check in the spirit of keeping the peace often transmit mixed and confusing messages to children. As we established in the previous chapter, even if children don't understand exactly what's happening around them, they're quite able to sense that there's *something* wrong. If you're angry and you try to act as though you're not, you leave children in conflict because what they're being told is at odds with what they're feeling.

As a grandparent raising your grandchildren, it may be uncomfortable for you to admit that you're in any way angry or resentful of the situation you're in. In the interest of doing what's best for your grandchildren, you try to keep a stiff upper lip, fearing that if you let on how aggravated you really are, you'll dash your whole image as a loving grandparent. Many of us have been misled by our belief that anger diminishes or poisons love, and we're never taught that love and anger can exist quite comfortably side by side. When we feel angry at people we love, we feel guilty. We secretly feel that being angry with them is bad-mannered or rude, and so we try not to show it. Isn't it odd, though, that in thinking this way we choose to believe that our so-called "bad" feelings are more powerful than our "good" ones?

If we can agree that there are really no good or bad feelings and that all feelings give us equally important cues about what's going on both inside and outside us, how then can anger be a more powerful force than love? Can it really be the case that anger is more _de_structive than love is _con_structive? Why then do we persist in believing that it's not okay for us to be angry with people we love? In so doing, we imply that anger destroys or diminishes love and that love lacks the same power over anger. Our comforting cliché, *"Love conquers all,"* seems to slip quietly away while we're busily wasting energy hiding the fact that someone we care about has irritated us. We forget very quickly that we can love and be angry with these people at the same time. In fact, it has been commonly said that those we love have the greatest ability to anger us.

Our feelings toward people we care about are obviously deeper than our feelings toward casual acquaintances. Family members push our buttons with more skill, more frequency, and more accuracy than others because they are usually the very people who installed them. As a rule, we don't tend to waste as much time getting worked up over people whose feelings and opinions aren't important to us (unless, of course, our ego is on the line).

Feeling guilty about being angry is not only a waste of energy, but it can also create even more tension where enough tension already exists. Grandparents who take on that labor of love of raising their grandchildren often feel enormously guilty if they find themselves in any way resentful of their duty. If they're uncomfortable with those feelings or are unable to accept their anger as a natural and expected part of the package, their efforts to hold it in may cause them to lash out inappropriately or unexpectedly at seemingly trivial things. Imagine the shock of the unassuming grandchild when his or her otherwise consistently warm and loving grandparent lapses into an angry tirade over some minor annoyance!

And then there are those who are so filled with negative feelings that they give their anger free reign. As a means of making others feel as awful as they themselves feel, they strike out harshly at every opportunity. These individuals use their angry outbursts to bully or intimidate others into doing as they're told.

Ironically, those who use such tactics as a means of gaining dominance or superiority never command the respect they're looking for. Instead, they inspire others to fear, mistrust, despise, and even avoid them altogether. Their use of force gives them a feeling of power, but their power is generally false because others see through it for what it really is—an attempt to bully others into paying attention. In truth, those who use such tactics lack the skill or patience to get their point across in a more effective way.

These individuals use their anger to put them at an unfair advantage over others by making the price for defying them very high. People who rule, govern, lead, or parent by intimidating or instilling fear in others are people who secretly doubt their own authority. Unconvinced that they'll be taken seriously or even listened to at all if they take a calm or rational approach, these people brandish their authority over others as a means of keeping them in line. Because of their chronically domineering manner or angry demeanor, others are reluctant to challenge or disobey them. Thus, their aggressive tactics appear to pay off because they get the desired result.

The truth of the matter, however, is that the only real power these people have lies in their position and not in their point. They threaten people with their power because they can't persuade them with their views. Bullies are rarely respected, and those who do obey them do so simply to avoid the backlash. The oppressed may not openly defy their oppressor, but they will always find a more subtle and deceptive way to rebel.

With respect to grandparents, anger in all of its forms is a typical response to the pressures and strains of their role. Its explosive form, erupting, for example, in physical violence, does exist but is very rare. It's much more common for these feelings to show themselves in less obvious ways, taking the form of sarcasm or other bitingly critical comments. For example, the weary grandparent who feels stretched to the limit and pulled in too many directions at once may snap at the grandchild who asks for something relatively simple like a new toy. The grandparent, struggling with the pressure of having to be everything to everyone, tries to hold back the emotional overload. Instead of flying into a rage, the grandparent delivers the anger in a neater package by using the comeback, *"Do you know how much that costs?"* which in its very tone is certainly an overreaction to the request. Overreacting by definition means that our reaction is out of proportion to the situation and should be a tip-off to us that we've been stockpiling our frustrations.

Overreacting in this way may seem less destructive than an all-out attack but will still leave others feeling taken aback. These and comebacks like them will startle the wide-eyed grandchild who has no advance warning of the grandparent's rising level of frustration. *"Do you know how much that costs?"* is an odd thing to bark at a child who has no concept of the value of money. The exhausted grandparent is too tired and fed up to form a more reassuring reply like, *"We just don't have the money for that right now, honey."*

The familiar battle cries of exasperated grandparents who carry the weight of the world on their shoulders often come in the form of phrases like, *"Why don't you ask your good-for-nothing mother or father to buy it for you!"* or, *"There are lots of things I'd like to have, too, you know."* And of course, we mustn't leave out the favorite: *"Get used to not getting everything you want."* And no one can forget that time-honored classic, the last resort of all emotionally and financially drained parents and grandparents, *"Do you think we're made of money?"* or its variation, *"Do you think money grows on trees?"* What these remarks all amount to is a misdirected release of tension and an attempt to put everyone on notice that the demands of raising a family are overwhelming.

Although such sarcastic comebacks may seem harmless enough, they deliver a stinging blow. The unspoken message for a child on the receiving end is, *"How dare you ask me for anything else!"* These exact words need never be spoken for this message to be clearly delivered.

Some of the most enduring messages we receive as children are those that are never spoken directly. No one ever had to tell us that we were appreciated, important, accepted, or wanted for us to know that this was the case—but by the same token, no one ever has to tell us that we're a nuisance, unimportant, unwanted, or burdensome for us to feel this way as well. As the adult here, you as a grandparent are doubly responsible, not just for the words you speak, but also for the way you speak them.

If we're willing to take an honest look at ourselves, we're forced to admit that quips like, *"Do you think we're made of money?"* and, *"Do you know how much that costs?"* are made entirely for effect and nothing more. Are we really asking the 8-year-old who wants a new bike to conduct a comparative market analysis or to present us with a well-researched feasibility study of how the family budget could accommodate the expense? Of course not! So why pose such questions at all?

Let's face it, such remarks are made for the adult's benefit—not the child's. They give the adults a spotlight to wave their banner of indignation and to show everyone just how overworked they really are. If all we want to tell children is that they might not be able to get what they are asking for, then what's the harm in stating this simply and directly? Sure, *"I'm sorry, but we can't afford it right now,"* doesn't pack nearly the punch the other statements do, but it does serve to deliver the answer of, *"no,"* with love and understanding.

Certainly sarcastic and biting remarks leave a lasting impression, but is it really the impression we want to leave? The danger is that these responses cause children to stop asking for what they need. The message they actually deliver can prove to be far more damaging than the message they were trying to convey. As children, we survive countless *"no's."* It's by no means the job of adults to protect children from these *"no's"* by giving them everything they want, but to teach them with love and understanding that *"no"* is a fact of life. We can't protect children from the disappointment of not getting what they want, but we can teach them how to handle this disappointment with dignity. In other words, we can't prevent the injury, but we can keep from adding insult to it.

For children, the tone we use, or the mood we convey leaves a more lasting impression than our actual words. Later in life, we're not likely to recall the specifics or recount verbatim what words were spoken to us as children, but don't underestimate a child's capacity to vividly remember the feelings the words carried with them. For example, children won't recall exactly what happened to cause mommy and daddy to divorce, but they'll recall vividly how they felt when they were told. Likewise, they won't recall what was said to them when they asked for a new bike or the latest game, but they will clearly recall that the response they got when they did ask left them wishing they hadn't.

Parents and grandparents alike have to be extremely conscious of the impression their statements leave on their (grand)children. While no one can avoid the occasional angry outburst, the impact over time of consistently angry or even sarcastic remarks will cause a child to stop asking for anything at all. A child exposed continuously to these kinds of messages is a child who will either shut down and withhold feelings altogether—unable, as an adult, to ask for what he or she needs—or a child who, as an adult, becomes even better at striking back in venomous ways.

The truth for grandparents may be that raising grandchildren is indeed burdensome, and that it places undue strain on already diminished resources. But it can't be stressed enough that this is neither the fault nor the problem of these children. No child should ever bear the burden of the choices or decisions made by an adult. You may not have chosen to bring these children into the world, but you *did* choose to accept the responsibility for their care. Therefore, the stresses and strains that raising this second family places on you were not of the children's choosing and are not their problem.

It's perfectly okay to let your grandchildren know that times are tough and that money is tight. And it's okay for them to know that they may not get everything they ask for. There is little harm in being straightforward. Doing so won't protect your grandchildren from the pain of not having everything they want or need, but it will spare them the humiliation and shame of feeling they're wrong for having wants and needs at all.

Reacting calmly and lovingly to a child's endless demands requires effort (and even a little self-restraint), but there's no better way to say *"no"* than with love. Long after these encounters, the words you have chosen will be lost in the mists of time, but their delivery will echo for years to come. The disappointment of not getting the latest toy or game is transient, and it passes as quickly as the fads themselves. Shame and embarrassment, however, do not pass with changes of fortune—they tend to grow deeper as the years go by.

Parents and grandparents are entitled to periodic bouts of exasperation—they come with the territory. But we're not entitled to bury a child with our adult-sized frustrations.

Unfavorable messages can be delivered with the ease and simplicity of favorable ones. The trick is to deliver them with as little emotional baggage attached as possible. The messages we give as adults will have no more significance to a child than we attach to them. A healthy, well-adjusted, and confident child can emerge from even the most desperate environment if the atmosphere is secure and loving enough. It's truly not our circumstances, but our way of approaching them, that determines whether we rise or fall in the face of adversity. Grandparents can't make up for what their grandchildren haven't got, but with a consistently loving approach, they can make what little they seem to have go a lot further.

Remember, it's the full-time job of a child to feel cared for and valued, to feel safe and protected, and to bask in the naive bliss of believing that there is no more important individual on the planet than that child. It is therefore the full-time challenge of any parent, and a particular challenge to any second-time parent, to skillfully manage the stresses and strains of raising a first or second set of children with calm consistency. It's the truly committed grandparent who can meet all of these demands while at the same time creating a home environment where the children can rest peacefully assured that, no matter what hardships and limitations the family faces, their basic needs will somehow be met. Comfort and a sense of fulfillment are not created by how much the parent or parent figure is able to provide, but rather by how much they're able to love. Patience and understanding are a grandparent's least expensive natural resources.

Suit Up, It's Time for Target Practice

In addition to the challenge of managing your own anger, you'll no doubt find yourself the generous recipient of more than your fair share of anger from others. Grandparents are the most likely safe targets for their grandchildren's ambivalent feelings toward their parents. If you can't pick on the one you want to target, just pick on whoever is available, right?

Depending on the age of the children at the time they're dropped off at their grandparent's door, they arrive already depressed, angry, resentful, frightened, mistrustful, or in overall emotional turmoil. The older the children, the more emotional baggage they'll have had a chance to collect and will no doubt pack for their journey to your home.

Children of alcohol- and drug-addicted parents, as well as children of parents who are unstable for other reasons, will bring with them more than their share of physical and emotional problems. Some have been born suffering the aftermath of parental chemical abuse, which can have a wide variety of long-lasting effects. These may take the form of physical disabilities, mental or emotional disturbances, or perceptual, learning, or attention deficits. So on top of becoming parents without preparation, the grandparents who inherit these children also inherit the legacy of the parent's poor judgments, negligence, impulsiveness, and indulgences.

Those children who escape physical damage often suffer emotional scars that are much deeper and more difficult to detect. Some emotional problems may be readily apparent, while others may not surface until later in the child's development. What all of these children have in common, however, is some form of simmering hostility toward what their parent has or has not done. This animosity may have many faces and may take many forms.

Some children trap their anger inside, blaming themselves for not being worthy of their parents' attention. These children will appear withdrawn, non-communicative, and forlorn. Others will channel their hostility outward in seemingly irrational and unpredictable ways. They may refuse to follow instructions, behave disrespectfully, or get in trouble for any number of rebellious or defiant acts. In any case, the grandparent inherits the challenge of striking a balance between flexibility and limit setting, between tolerance and discipline, and between psychology and good, old-fashioned common sense. But, how do you create a safe and nurturing environment when there's so much conflict in the air?

Children whose parents have not been around to listen or who have made it unsafe for them to express themselves openly often vent their bottled up feelings on the closest targets—their grandparents. In this case, it's the next in line who's held accountable for the parents' failure to provide. The children may accuse the grandparents of running the parents out of their lives, or even blame the grandparents for meddling and driving a wedge between the parents and their children. In short, they're angry with the grandparents simply for not being their parents. It's only human for us all to feel angry when we're being hurt in some way. You have now become the heir to the child's pain. Your best approach at this point is not to remove yourself from the line of fire but to suit up appropriately for battle. Uncomfortable as it my be, you can't discourage children from expressing their feelings, but you can help them fine-tune their communication skills so that they learn more appropriate ways of expressing them.

If you're a person who's uncomfortable with your own anger, it will be doubly difficult for you to tolerate your grandchildren's anger, especially when it's aimed directly at you. If you've bought into the idea that anger diminishes love, then you're likely to believe that it's disrespectful for children to show anger toward adults, most especially parent-type adults. The danger here is that you're then likely to make the mistake of interpreting your grandchildren's outbursts as a slap in the face.

Although no parent or parent figure should tolerate blatant disrespect, be aware that the open expression of anger is not in itself disrespectful. If you automatically equate a child showing anger with a child showing disrespect, you'll discourage such expressions, and you may even be tempted to go so far as to punish your grandchildren when they're rightfully angry. Your misunderstandings about the purpose of anger have now led you to feel attacked and demeaned by your unappreciative grandchildren who are merely confused, in pain, and desperately in need of your support.

Your misinterpretation of their behavior, in turn, causes you to shut them down, making them angrier and more resentful of you. By viewing their anger as a personal attack or a display of disrespect, you not only miss what they're really trying to tell you, but you also double the level of animosity in your home. Were you trying to make things better or worse?

Punishing children for expressing anger will only intensify it. When a child cries, *"I hate you!"* this kind of outburst should never be taken literally, because it doesn't have the same meaning to a child as it does to an adult. Offended by their child's blatant lack of consideration, a parent or grandparent's most common reflex is to reprimand the child with, *"Don't ever say a thing like that!"* Such rebuts close the lines of communication and rarely achieve the desired result. Feeling hit below the belt, the (grand)parent's aim in responding has shifted from hearing the child out to correcting the wrongdoing.

It's extraordinarily difficult in these situations to keep your cool and allow the lines of communication to stay open when your feelings are being hurt. But when we shout, *"Don't ever say a thing like that,"* what we're really telling a child is that it's not okay to get angry at us.

By training yourself to listen more closely to the child's real message than to how it's being delivered, you can keep the lines of communication open by avoiding getting your feelings hurt in the first place. Becoming more comfortable with your own angry feelings, and learning that it's possible to express them in inoffensive ways, makes you more of a teacher than a disciplinarian. When you make the mistake of striking back, you lose an opportunity for more meaningful conversation or a chance to show the child that when we're angry at someone, it's important to tell the person and to do so in a nonthreatening way.

The most effective way to encourage openness without encouraging disrespect from angry children is to offer them a more appropriate way of expressing themselves. We are too quick to tell them when they're in the wrong without offering a more appropriate alternative. It's difficult for anyone at any age to stop doing something that's become comfortable and familiar without being shown another way of doing it. The most effective responses for (grand)parents are ones that acknowledge children's feelings, inform them that their way of expressing themselves could hurt someone else's feelings, and offer them a means of getting their point across in a way that would be easier for others to hear.

Example #1:
Child: *"I hate you!"*
Counterattack:
Grandparent: *"Don't ever say a terrible thing like that!"*
Constructive Alternative Responses:
Grandparent: *"I understand that you're upset, but saying what you said can hurt peoples' feelings. I'd like to know why you feel so mad at me, so let's talk about it rather than have a shouting match."*

Or:

Grandparent: *"You must be really upset to say that you hate me. Sometimes when we're really hurt we say things we don't mean. When you're calmer, I'd like to know what I did to make you so mad so we can find a way to make up."*

Example #2:
Child: *"Why don't you just go away... I wish you were dead!"*
Counterattack:
Grandparent: *"Oh, really? Well, maybe I will die, and then you'll really be sorry!"*
Constructive Alternative Responses:
Grandparent: *"It would really hurt me to think you meant what you said. If I've upset you, I'd like you to tell me so, rather than saying something I know you don't really mean."*
Or:

Grandparent: *"It really hurts me to hear you say that. Sometimes when I feel that mad, what I really feel is scared. Maybe you're afraid I'll leave you someday, too, and you want me to just go away and get it over with. I can understand that."*

If you're a grandparent raising grandchildren, fasten your emotional safety belt. Get accustomed to anger and all of its variations, and accept it as a part of the child's natural healing process. Make friends with it and learn to use its power to your advantage in constructive, rather than destructive, ways. Counterattacks certainly show children who's the boss, but they leave them with the feeling that you're yet another person they can't trust. Angry children are hurting children. Don't get so caught up in reprimanding them for their unpolished communication skills that you miss what they're really trying to say. Children who have been with a less-than-enthusiastic parent will in all likelihood have missed out on the experience of being taught how to express themselves more effectively. Not only will they be unpracticed at talking about what they feel, but they'll probably also have very little faith that anyone is really interested in hearing what they have to say. Remember, these are the same children who have had their parents' ineffective coping skills to use as their only guide. Keep your expectations realistic. Your job is not to admonish them for what they haven't yet learned, but to help them unlearn their old, defensive ways of coping and replace them with healthier, more effective alternatives.

The Best Defense...

Never respond to a child's anger by becoming angry or defensive in return. Understand that becoming defensive is our natural way of responding to a perceived attack. Because anger directed at us is perceived as an attack, it will naturally trigger our urge to defend ourselves. Our defense systems are automatic and will be set in motion whether an impending attack is physical or verbal, life-threatening, or merely annoying. Our defense systems aren't able to distinguish the kind of attack they sense—they're too busy protecting us to care. Whether verbal or physical, direct or implied, in the eyes of our defenses, a threat is a threat is a threat. We can't turn off our impulse to protect and defend ourselves—it's automatic. We can, however, choose whether or not we act on it.

It's human to *want* to defend ourselves when we're being attacked, but it takes skill to decide if the threat really warrants defensive action. When anyone (even a child) throws hostility at you, you'll be tempted to defend yourself with a counterattack. But, if there's any hope of establishing your grandchildren's trust in the face of confusion, you'll have to resist this temptation at all cost.

When two individuals of any age lash out at one another in anger, any communication will be hopelessly lost in the commotion. Once begun, this kind of warfare deteriorates into a game of win or lose where there's no real strategic advantage in hearing the other person's point of view. In this kind of confrontation, the goal is to *win*, not to *understand.*

When both parties are adults, each bears equal responsibility for either keeping the battle going or for calling it off. When one party is a child, we as the adult bear full responsibility for calling off the battle by flatly refusing to fight. Remember, no fight can continue unless both sides are willing to participate.

Initially, it takes patience and self-control to resist matching anger with anger in return. But once mastered, the results of your new approach will be much more rewarding. To avoid reacting on impulse requires more effort in that we have to tune in more to the message behind the words than to the words themselves. With children (and adults who occasionally act like children), you need to reach beneath the words they hurl at you to uncover what they're feeling but just don't have the savvy to say.

Anger is often a disguise for pain. By refusing to be detoured by the anger, and by responding directly to the pain, you show the children that you aren't fooled by their bluster because you're hip to what's really going on inside them. If you speak to the hurt and ignore the anger, the anger often goes away on its own. Anger is usually smoke from a deeper fire— blowing it away doesn't put out the flames.

Example #1:

Child: *"You're not my mother!"*

Counterattack:

Grandparent: *"I may not be your mother, but if it weren't for me, you'd be in a foster home."*

Constructive Alternative Responses:

Grandparent: *"It must hurt a lot not to have your mother and father here to help you with this."* (Re-sponds to the <u>hurt</u>, not the anger.)

Or:

Grandparent: *"You really miss your mom, don't you?"* (Addresses the <u>loss</u>.)

Example #2:

Child: *"What do you care? I'm only here because my mom dumped me on you!"*

Counterattack:

Grandparent: *"Don't you think I know that? I obviously care more about you than she does."*

Constructive Alternative Response:

Grandparent: *"I'm sorry you've had to be shuffled around. It's hard not knowing where you belong or if anyone really cares, but*

you know I took you in because I love you, not because I had to."
(Responds to the <u>abandonment</u>, not the accusation.)

There are no appropriate or inappropriate emotions, just appropriate and inappropriate ways of expressing or dealing with them. You have to believe this first yourself in order to teach this to your grandchildren. Stay calm and objective, and avoid taking their outbursts to heart. When they shout, *"You're not my mother!"* they're not telling you anything you both don't already know. So maybe there's another reason for the remark. Was it intended to hurt you? I don't think so. It's more a comment about the conspicuous absence of a parent. More often than not, these statements are about what the children are missing, not what they got in exchange.

It's natural for children to test you in every possible way. They're checking to see if you'll throw them away, too. They also want to see how much you're willing to tolerate, particularly if there were no limits or restrictions put on them by their absent or permissive parent. By acting out in these ways, they're often searching for limits that will provide them with a sense of security. It may be difficult to understand why children seek out limits only to rebel against them, but for these children, lashing out is the only way they know of checking to see if anyone is paying attention. In pushing against your limits, they're testing to see if restrictions will be put on them, and if those restrictions will be consistently enforced.

By responding with love and reassurance, you can provide a sense of security and perhaps give your grandchildren, for the first time in their lives, the chance to experience that the limits surrounding them can be trusted and are not subject to change without notice. Troubled children are not bad children in search of discipline, but rather lost children in search of direction. The way you respond to them will determine if your role in their lives will be that of a warden or that of a teacher.

6

Parenting Two Generations at One Time

There is no denying that the challenges facing those who take on the commitment of raising a second family are numerous and far-reaching. These challenges begin with the very basics, like considering the costs and juggling a budget and expenses in order to afford such a proposition. And then they rapidly escalate into broader social considerations, like how to explain your living arrangement to others, where to go for help or support, and how to effectively fend off the barrage of advice and opinions you'll get from well-meaning family and friends. These logistical challenges come together with the more complex and daunting task of taking care of yourself both emotionally and physically while sifting through the deep and confusing pile of emotions the whole situation has left you with.

As if to complicate matters even further, grandparents raising grandchildren face a dual challenge: they have to find a way to become parents to their newly acquired children while at the same time continuing a parent-child relationship with their own adult children. What this all amounts to is that these grandparents take on the formidable task of parenting two generations at once. As if just being a parent weren't enough trouble!

As members of a larger family unit, each of us plays several roles simultaneously; whether it be husband or wife, son or daughter, aunt or uncle, brother or sister. And outside the family, we are all part of a larger social and community network where we play still more roles as employee, school board member, choir director, Boy Scout/Girl Scout leader, secretary of the local fundraising organization...and the list goes on. Our lives are complex enough without being caught in the middle of an intergenerational trap.

In the previous chapter we identified issues and strategies for managing problem situations that arise when grandchildren who feel cast aside by their parents rebel against their new caregivers. In this chapter, we turn the generational focus to the other side and take a look at difficult parents whose problems have become their children's while continuing to confound their own parents, who have now become grandparents along the way. Being parent to two generations at once puts a further drain on these grandparents' ever-dwindling energy, patience, time, and other resources.

Grandparents who inherit their grandchildren when a parent has died have a challenge of a different kind as the family begins to reassemble itself in the wake of such a loss. But a son or daughter whose questionable or spontaneous lifestyle has followed him or her into adulthood and now into parenthood presents an ongoing series of dilemmas to those who have become grandparents in the process. Grandparents who must raise a grandchild while continuing a life-long battle as parents to an adult problem child feel hopelessly tangled up in a never-ending saga of conflicts, uncertainty, crisis, and emotional mayhem. In this chapter, we'll look at some of the most common struggles and conflicts that arise between parents and grandparents when a child is caught in the middle.

It is certainly a given that not all parents who place their children in their grandparents' care are troubled individuals afflicted with chronic personal problems, but it's a cold, harsh reality that many are. This chapter is not intended as a global condemnation of these parents; it is included for the sake of those weary grandparents whose adult children continue to try their patience, blame and manipulate them, and create such conflict and confusion in their lives that they're often left questioning their own mental stability. As a parent, it will be natural for you to instinctively want what's best for your children. And if one or more of these children stray down an undesirable or destructive path, you will no doubt find yourself accepting some or all of the blame for their misdeeds. You may be all too familiar with that self-doubting voice in your head that tells you that your children would not have made such poor choices had you been a better parent.

As interconnecting parts of a caring family unit, parents naturally take on their children's struggles as their own. If you are a parent, this is already glaringly obvious to you. It would be impossible for anyone to rest idly in the background while someone they love wanders into harm's way. Although it would be impossible to simply switch off the pain you feel when loved ones go astray, it is entirely possible for you to learn how to resist the overpowering urge to step in and set them straight. To do so requires that you recognize that it's your own parental guilt that is making you feel it's your duty to help. If you feel your faulty parenting is to blame for your children's poor choices as adults, you won't be able to resist the temptation to volunteer when clean-up time arrives. But by doing so, the more important function you serve is the one of now supporting your adult children's unwillingness to take responsibility for their own decisions and behaviors. And as you will soon see, you've also armed your adult children with a convenient weapon that they'll later use against you.

This parental guilt, as we discussed in Chapter 3, can become the most powerful weapon adult children have at their disposal. When wielded in the direction of their parents, it allows them to dodge taking responsibility for themselves and hold their parents liable for whatever trouble they've gotten themselves into. Keeping the torrent of blame flowing in the direction of their parents gives these adult children a blanket disclaimer covering the chaotic state of their lives while conveniently making them completely powerless to do anything to change it. If someone else is always to blame for their problems, then someone else holds the key to solving them. In this case, that "someone else" is you.

Your best hope of disentangling yourself from this snarl of guilt, blame, and responsibility is to call upon some concepts we covered in Chapter 3. Remember the difference between understanding and blame? Now is the time to put it to use.

Even if you've played a role in setting the stage for the lives your adult children are living, *understand* the part you've played, and *understand* that in spite of it, you are in no way to *blame*. The belief that you are to blame is the vulnerability your adult children have used to keep you in this place. By blaming yourself for your children's troubles, you give them your blessing to remain in a child-like state of helplessness, neither responsible for their problems nor able to solve them. As a parent with responsibility-dodging, blame-seeking children, believe me when I say, you'll get all of the blame and none of the credit. If you have adult children whose only inspiration to pick up the phone to call you is their need for something, watch out—you've already been trapped. To get out, one of you has to stop playing this game. And given that there's much more in it for your children than there is for you, you can bank on the fact that it won't be them.

This kind of blame game requires that both children and parents play, or it won't work. You can't stop your adult children from trying to blame or manipulate you—being able to do so successfully has a tremendous payoff and is well worth the effort. What you will discover is that, while you can't stop them from trying, if you learn the rules of the manipulation game, you can see it when it starts and choose whether or not you care to play. Only when manipulation stops paying off will the manipulator eventually stop using it. Once you are savvy to the rules of the game, it will be extremely difficult for the manipulator to continue being successful—for the most part, you can't lure a knowledgeable victim into an obvious trap.

What follows is a list of common manipulative tactics that are favored by adult children who have an investment in placing their parents at fault for their own actions. You will find that most of these tactics rely on the parents' sense of responsibility or guilt. Study them, become familiar with them, and you'll be able to spot them immediately, instead of realizing too late that you've once again been duped. But above all, remain abundantly clear that your only goal here is to stop playing the game and begin putting the responsibility for your children's lives back where it belongs—in their own hands.

Never approach this subject with the goal of getting your adult children to admit or even see that they are trying to manipulate you. The skill of manipulation can become as instinctive as the will to survive; and of the many who successfully use it, most aren't even aware that what they are doing could be called manipulation.

Avoid engaging in further disputes or disagreements over how your children and you see their behavior differently. If you know you're being manipulated, that's all that's important. Remember that the payoff for manipulating someone in this way is ultimately the avoidance of responsibility. Could you reasonably expect the very people who live their lives avoiding responsibility to be open to accepting responsibility for being manipulative?

Six Common Manipulations and How to Avoid Them

1. Finger pointing

This is just as it sounds. While it's easy to understand in concept, it's not always so easily recognized in practice, due to the clever disguises it can wear. As with all of these manipulations, this one in particular depends on your guilt to pay off. Those who use this technique are likely to be those who are acutely in tune to your doubts about being a good parent or other areas of personal vulnerability. They see these as valuable weak points in your defensive armor and will not hesitate to use them to their advantage.

Examples of finger pointing

Your unmarried 22-year-old daughter, whose 2- and 3-year-old children now live with you, has just informed you that she's pregnant for a third time. You heave an exhausted sigh and once again try to draw her attention to her unmistakable inability to care for the children she already has. She, in turn, responds with one of the following statements:
- *"You can't blame me if I'm a bad parent—I had you as a role model."*
- *"How dare you criticize me. Look what you did!"*

* *"You think I have problems—look at how you raised me. You're the one who needs help."*

As you can clearly see, this tactic diverts attention from your daughter's (mis)behavior and turns it back to her favorite subject—you. By throwing you off balance, this strategy begs you to defend yourself and sets you up to trade places with her as the subject of the discussion. But you'll feel the need to defend yourself only if you forget the simple fact that no one can blame you for something you're not responsible for...that is, unless you *think* you're really responsible for it.

To illustrate this, imagine that your son were to accuse you of taking $20 from his wallet. In your right mind you'd never take $20 from him, even if he gave it to you, let alone take it without his knowing. In your own defense, you need to do no more than state that this just isn't your style and that it's more likely he forgot spending it. When you're certain of the truth, there's no need for elaborate explanation, justification, or convincing.

If, however, in response to the accusation, you were to lapse into a lengthy account of your whereabouts, his whereabouts, the wallet's whereabouts, and how this just couldn't possibly have happened, you begin to arouse suspicion about your innocence. The simple truth requires no justification, and those who feel the need to convince others of their innocence usually have something to hide. If you're guilty in some way, or if you just *feel* guilty (for other sneaky things you may have done), you'll crumble in response to the accusation and become hopelessly tangled up in pleading your case.

You will react to finger pointing statements only if you feel there is some merit to them. If you secretly believe you are to blame for your adult children's problems, this becomes a convenient button for them to push, which, with 100% accuracy, launches you into a tired rendition of, *"I did the best I could."* If this is the case, the manipulation is working beautifully by giving your children a swift and effective way to shift the focus of any critical discussion back to you. By allowing yourself to be put on the defense, you lose the offensive advantage, and in losing the offensive advantage, your discussion mysteriously shifts from whatever behavior you had been attempting to address and once again you are forced to defend your parental prowess. Sound exhausting? These kinds of discussions usually are.

Your best chance at defeating this manipulative technique is to regain the offensive position. Resisting the urge to argue with or correct your children's critical or accusatory statements prevents them from shifting the focus onto you. Even if you feel that somewhere in the hail of gunfire your children have made a valid point, simply acknowledge their point and quickly refocus the discussion. Their greatest power lies in baiting you into defending yourself.

Sample Responses

You could respond to your pregnant daughter's finger pointing statements with one of the following reactions:

- *"You're right. I have made my share of mistakes as a parent, but this is about you right now, not me."*
- *"I'm sorry if some of the things I've done have hurt you in some way, but it's high time for you to move on and start taking responsibility for your own choices now."*
- *"You're right. I do have problems of my own, and I might need to deal with them; but right now my biggest concern is you."*

Never strike back in response to finger pointing statements with such guilt inducing counterattacks as:

- *"I did the best I could, and I'm sorry you don't think it's good enough."*
- *"The biggest mistake I ever made was believing in you!"*

These comebacks do no more than let your children know that they've struck a nerve and that their finger pointing has worked. By being defensive or attacking in kind, you'll only support their position that they are victims. In these situations, your best defense is no defense at all.

2. The "if...then" evasion

In this tactic, manipulators make their actions contingent upon yours, and in so doing, succeed in making you the one responsible for the outcome. In other words, you are put in a position in which you hold the power to determine what other people do. This tactic links their actions inextricably to whatever course of action you choose, holding you personally accountable for any consequence that befalls them.

When this manipulation works, the manipulators back you into a corner by convincing you that you're the one who's backing them into a corner. It's as if you're forcing them to do something they wouldn't otherwise choose to do.

Examples of the "if...then" evasion
- *"If you tell the social worker about Sarah's bruises, I'll lose my visitation with her. They'll make me go back to counseling, and I'll end up having to quit my job to make all those appointments. I'll be right back where I started—is that what you wanted?"*
- *"If you make me stop drinking completely, I'll have no way to unwind. You know how much stress I'm under. What if I go off on someone and do something really stupid. Then how would you feel?"*
- *"If you say I have to go back to rehab just to take my own kid for a day, I just won't come around anymore at all. How will it feel when you have to explain to her why you won't let me see her?"*

There is a not-so-subtle threatening undertone to these kinds of statements. They clearly imply that what you are doing is tying your children's hands and stripping them of their options. This leaves them with no other course of action but a destructive or unhealthy one. The underlying message here is, *"If you make me do something I don't want to do, you'll be sorry."* And the message you receive loud and clear from this, which makes this approach so highly effective, is, *"If something bad comes of this, it will be on your head."*

When you take it at its most basic level, this manipulation counts on you to buy into the ridiculous presumption that there is only one possible way for the manipulator to go. *"If you do x, I'll be forced to do y."* If you yield to the hidden threat here, you'll be led to feel that your expectation/action *(x)* is unreasonable and that it will inevitably result in disaster *(y)*. You feel forced to back down from your stance in order to prevent the threat from being carried out...and then being blamed for it.

The most effective way to dismantle this manipulation is to take the teeth out of these threats. This is best accomplished by drawing attention to the absurdity of the notion that there is only one way the manipulator can respond to the situation. You have to poke a hole in the manipulator's basic premise that *x* can only result in *y*. By understanding that *x* doesn't necessarily have to lead to *y* (there is always more than one choice), you break the deadly link between your action and their proposed reaction.

If there is no cause-effect relationship, there is no manipulation. Your best response to the *"if...then"* evasion is to state the obvious, which is that your action doesn't have the power to dictate your children's reaction. If you do *x* and they choose to do *y*, then that's on them. They always have choices. After all, there is never just one course of action we can take at any given time.

Sample Responses

- *"I have to do whatever I can to protect my grandchild, and if my calling the social worker has consequences for you, this is not my doing. What you've done has forced me to take this action. If you'd have made better choices, then you wouldn't have to worry about being reported."*
- *"I'm sorry you feel you have no other option than to do something stupid. It seems there should be other ways for you to deal with this."*
- *"Being off drugs is an option for you and it's not an unreasonable one for me to ask. If you choose not to go to rehab to be able to take Sarah for the day, you'll need to take responsibility for the choice you've made and stop putting it on me. Staying away altogether is only hurting her for something you're not willing to do."*

3. Generalization

In this technique, manipulators paint their world with a very broad brush, creating an *"all or nothing"* impression of any given situation. Extreme adjectives such as *"always"* and *"never"* are enlisted to distort the impact of a single incident, making it seem much more significant than it really is. One occurrence becomes the rule, thus raising the stakes to a level out of proportion to the actual situation. Being drawn into this brand of logic will cause you to lose sight of the real issue because you've been thrown off base by the exaggeration.

The trick of this tactic is that the manipulator is subtly and strategically able to lure you into thinking that you are the one who is overreacting by suddenly turning the tables on you. For example, if you have ever caught someone in an inconsistency and confronted them with it only to be accused of calling them a *"liar,"* you already have experience with this manipulation. Chances are that before you were even aware of what had happened, their indignation sparked by being called a liar caused you to feel guilty about having called into question the person's good character. This causes you to think that certainly you must have overreacted to the inconsistency since the person seems so badly wounded by your questioning. And chances are that the encounter ended with you either apologizing for having hurt the person's feelings, or with you defending yourself in a futile attempt to convince the accused that what you said was not really what you meant at all. If either was the case, the manipulation worked perfectly.

When effective, this tactic allows the perpetrator to skirt the issue by exaggerating your point, thus making you feel you've been unfair or overly judgmental. You are once again placed on the defense, and your discussion turns from the inappropriateness of the other person's behavior to the inappropriateness of your reaction.

Examples of generalization

• Mother: *"I'd like you to be on time when you pick up Sarah on Sundays so that I'm not late for church again."*

Daughter: *"Nothing I ever do is good enough for you! You're always putting me down like I'm some sort of loser who can't get her act together. You make it sound like I've got nothing to do all day but make sure you get to church on time."*

Mother: *"That's not what I meant...of course I don't think you're a loser. I'm proud of what you've done. Maybe I am overreacting. A few minutes is no big deal. I'm sorry if I hurt your feelings."*

Another example

•   Mother: *"When you make promises to come over and spend time with Sarah, I expect you to keep your word. I don't like this making plans and not following through on them. It's not fair to her."*

Daughter: *"You never give me credit for what I do. All you do is criticize me when I make the slightest little mistake. You're not satisfied with anything I do. Not everyone is perfect like you, you know."*

Mother: *"Of course I'm not perfect, but you don't seem to understand what I'm saying. All I meant was, try to be a bit more considerate. Is that asking too much? Geez, I'm sorry I even brought it up."*

In dealing with this manipulation, beware of the exaggerations and avoid falling into a clever trap like the mother in our examples. Keep in mind that what the other person is hearing is not really what you've said. This does not mean that the person's perception of what you're saying is wrong; it simply means it's been distorted to serve a specific end. The perception has to be slanted to match the hidden agenda of avoiding the admission of any wrongdoing.

If you understand that this is a reception problem and not a transmission problem, you'll be less tempted to invest a lot of energy into rephrasing what you've said ad nauseam in an attempt to finally get the other person to hear it the way you meant it. If you have phrased your request or feelings in a clear, accurate, and nonaccusatory manner, and a generalization or exaggeration is reflected back to you, you can rest assured that the distortion was not your doing. Don't get caught up in the unproductive game of, *"What you heard is not what I said,"* or you will again find yourself on the defense, and the real issue will be lost. Stick to your point, stay with the facts, and avoid reacting to the exaggeration.

Sample Responses

- Mother: *"It's obvious that you feel put down, but I don't quite get how my asking you to be on time means I've called you a loser—that's quite a leap! We're just talking about your promptness here, not your total worth as a human being."*
- Mother: *"I know you always feel criticized when I bring this up, but let's please try not to make it more than it really is. We're talking about courtesy and responsibility here, not perfection or imperfection. I don't need you to be perfect, I would just like to see some improvement."*

Resist the temptation to defend yourself against the allegation that you've judged or criticized your children in some way—but also be sensitive to their feelings. Their distorted perception will cause them to <u>feel</u> judged or criticized even when there was nothing the least bit critical or judgmental about what you said. You can acknowledge their feelings without agreeing with their viewpoint. Doing so will foil their attempts to make you out to be the enemy.

If you remain understanding and impartial, the *"you against me"* quality of this manipulation is thwarted. After all, it's harder for people to maintain that you're out to get them when you're sympathetic to their feelings. In order for this manipulation to succeed, the manipulators must bait you into feeling that you are working against them so that they can act wounded. The hurt they claim you have inflicted on them is then used to make you feel guilty, and it's this guilt that is the mechanism that puts you on the defensive. And as long as you are on the defensive, they succeed once again in avoiding responsibility for their own behavior.

4. *The bluff*

This form of manipulation causes you to confuse intentions with actions and tries to convince you that both are deserving of equal credit. When used effectively, *"the bluff"* draws you away from whatever has or has not been done by the manipulator and asks you to accept the notion that sincere effort or desire outweighs actual results. This manipulation makes it very difficult for you to hold the person accountable for what he or she did or did not do because of its assumption that the actual outcome doesn't matter if it was not done deliberately.

With this in mind, beware of the use of the word *trying*. This key word is always a dead giveaway that this particular brand of logic is at play. In essence, it's saying, *"Of course I didn't do it, but at least I tried."* To more clearly understand the power of this kind of thinking, consider for a moment your own use of it. Many of us unknowingly use *trying* as an excuse for not actually accomplishing what we've set out to accomplish. When falling short of a goal we have set, the phrase, *"I tried,"* speaks volumes. It makes us feel better by allowing us to cash in on our efforts and excusing our lack of results. By giving ourselves credit for our efforts in this manner, we allow ourselves to experience equal satisfaction for our efforts and our accomplishments.

Although it may seem innocent enough, this way of thinking can quietly lull us into a false sense of complacency by allowing, *"I tired"* to take the place of, *"I really did it."* Without realizing, we have created for ourselves a safe and convenient cop-out for our lack of results by allowing ourselves a sense of accomplishment even when we've accomplished nothing at all. By becoming aware of our own tendency to rationalize our behavior in this way, we are much more likely to spot it when others try to use it on us.

A second prominent phrase used in this kind of thinking is, *"I meant to/didn't mean to..."* Again, this style of logic beckons us to excuse an action in lieu of its intent. And again, equal credit is demanded for intentions and actions. If we are in fact guilty of justifying what we do in this same way, we're first in need of fine-tuning our own thinking before being able to effectively call other people on theirs.

When this manipulative hardball is thrown your way, stand firm in your understanding that intentions in no way excuse behavior. Believe that it is our actions and not our intentions that ultimately define our character. When someone hurts you, knowing that it wasn't done deliberately is not in itself sufficient to relieve the pain you feel. Even if someone didn't mean to hurt you, you hurt, just the same.

It's a fact that we as social creatures will inevitably hurt one another without intending to from time to time. But, as both caring and rational beings, we should be able to acknowledge what we have done and take whatever steps are necessary to ensure that we don't do it again. Beware of those who refuse to take responsibility for having hurt you, if even unintentionally, and who would have you believe that your feelings are not justified if the hurt was not purposefully inflicted. The fact of the matter is that most of the hurt we feel and cause others is done unintentionally. That we didn't mean to do it doesn't make us any less responsible for the fact that we did– –nor does it excuse us from acknowledging the hurt we've caused and taking measures to make sure we don't hurt the person in the same way again. Beware of those who use, *"I didn't mean to hurt you,"* to say, *"You don't have a right to feel the pain."*

Examples of "the bluff"
• *"So what if I still party on the weekends; you don't expect me to stop living, do you? I'm going to those meetings like you wanted, I'm not going overboard like I used to, and I'm really trying this time. You should be happy for me instead of putting me down just because I don't live up to your standards. If you're going to nag me even when I'm doing better, I might as well quit the meetings and go back to what I was doing before."*

(In this example, the effort of going to meetings is expected to excuse the fact that the person's behavior has not actually changed.)

• *"I don't know why you're making such a big deal about my forgetting Sarah's recital. I have a lot on my mind. For God's sake, you make it sound like I do these things on purpose just to hurt her. What kind of person do you think I am, anyway?"*

(This statement asks the listener to overlook the hurt the behavior has caused in light of the fact that it wasn't intentional. In essence, *"I didn't mean to,"* is expected to make up for, *"I did."* Note how this manipulation subtly implies that not only is the other people's hurt unjustified, but it goes so far as to suggest that their hurt is an insult to the perpetrator.)

- *"You know I didn't mean to upset Sarah when I slammed the door on you the other day. She needs to learn not to be so sensitive. After all, everyone knows I have a problem with my temper. And you know what happens when you nag me like that."*

(This example allows the manipulator to avoid taking responsibility for unacceptable behavior by leading others to believe that they caused it. Instead of changing behavior, the manipulator is suggesting that it's the others' problem if they can't handle it. It's saying, *"I shouldn't have to stop hurting you; you should just get used to it."*)

Most statements that capture this manipulative tone succeed ultimately in shifting the focus from the manipulators and onto another person (usually you). The spotlight is turned from their behavior to others' reactions, giving the impression that the reaction, not the inappropriate behavior, is really the problem.

So while you're busy trying to decide whether or not you've really overreacted, as they would have you believe, what they did in the first place gets hopelessly lost in the confusion. As with the other tactics, be wary of this shift taking place so that you can either become skilled at preventing it from happening or quickly refocus the discussion as soon as you're aware that you've been sidetracked. Stand up for your feelings with the understanding that whenever someone acts in a hurtful way toward you, your hurt is a natural and expected result, regardless of whether the hurt was intentional or not. If you allow someone to convince you that your feelings are unwarranted, you permit them to escape responsibility for their actions. This is likely to be a person who will go on hurting you over and over again in the same manner. Don't let this kind of person off the hook so easily. What people *meant to do* or *didn't mean to do* never excuses what they *did*.

Sample Responses

• *"My expectation has always been that you stop "partying" altogether. Going to those meetings is supposed to help you learn how to do it. If you're going and still using, then obviously 'trying' isn't enough. Maybe it's your motivation and not the meetings that's the culprit here."*

• *"Whether or not you hurt Sarah on purpose is irrelevant. The point is, when you forget about her activities, it upsets her. I would certainly hope you don't do these things on purpose, but you need to understand that, whether or not it was intentional, you weren't there, and that hurts."*

• *"That you don't mean to hurt anyone with your temper doesn't make up for the fact that you keep doing it. Once the damage is done, it's done. I'd like to see you make more of an effort to prevent these blow-ups, instead of putting all the energy into making excuses for why you keep having them."*

5. Using the child to block

As its name suggests, this particular tactic is unique to circumstances in which two parties are at odds and the welfare of a child is at stake. With your situation, you must be wary of your adult children's tendency to slip their children into discussions merely to block themselves from fire. The fact that you care so deeply for your grandchildren gives your adult children a handy weapon. They are able to strike a sensitive emotional cord just by throwing a child's name into a heated discussion. And just by calling into question your concern for the welfare of this child, they uncover a convenient and highly effective button that, when pushed, disarms you when the heat has been turned up on them.

This strategy takes unfair advantage of your greatest area of vulnerability—your concern for your grandchild—and hits you where it hurts the most. When it is used effectively, one message will come through loud and clear, *"If you really cared about your grandchild, you wouldn't..."* Like the other techniques discussed here, it diverts attention from the real subject and onto someone or something else. This strategy is highly effective and difficult to detect because the *"someone or something else"* in this case happens to be your concern for the family. When it's being used on you, this manipulation will cause you to feel that you'd be a cruel and heartless person, a disgrace to grandparents everywhere, if you dared follow through with whatever line of thought or action you've proposed.

Examples of using the child to block
- *"Where do you get the nerve to call me inconsiderate? You're the inconsiderate one! Look what happens every time I come to get Sarah—you make up some hogwash about me looking like I'm high and you won't let me see her. Who is the inconsiderate one? If you really loved Sarah, you'd have more compassion for her, and you'd let her see me."*
- *"What do you mean I can't use the car anymore? I can't believe you're being so heartless. What's Sarah going to think? If you don't trust me, how's she ever going to learn to trust me—you're ruining any chance I have with her. You're trying to turn her against me."*
- *"I don't understand how you can say I shouldn't go out with my friends when I want. You expect my life to stop just because I had a kid?! I'd think you'd want Sarah to have a mother who's happy and has a life. Sure, I could sit home like you and twiddle my thumbs all the time, but then I'd be miserable. I guess what you really want is for Sarah to have a mother who's lonely and has no life...like you."*

These assertions may be clever, but they're completely without merit. They put in place a fictitious idea that your expectations of the parent could prove potentially damaging to the child. If you accept this idea, it becomes impossible for you to pursue your line of expectation without feeling like you're betraying the best interest of, or even doing emotional damage to, your grandchild. The parent again escapes unscathed. Very clever.

If you recognize this set-up, you can easily avoid it by flatly dismissing the false premise at its base. This premise connects your stance with a damaging consequence to your grandchild (who, by the way, had not even been a factor in the discussion before). By preventing this connection from being made, or breaking the connection as soon as you spot it, you undermine your adult child's attempt to hide behind your grandchild. You can then refocus on the real issue, which is the adult's behavior as an adult, separate from the child.

Sample Responses

• *"There's just no way you'll be able to convince me that spending time with Sarah when you're high is okay, so don't even try. Whether or not you get to see her depends entirely on you, not me. If you were able to be a bit more responsible, you'd understand that there are consequences to the choices we make. One consequence to your choice to continue getting high is not getting to spend as much time with Sarah."*

• *"I'm sorry that you feel my asking you to be more responsible with the car is heartless. Trust and respect are things we all have to earn, and your first step toward earning them is to start being more trustworthy and acting a bit more respectably. That way, you'd stop putting me in the position of having to be the bad guy who seems to always be on your case."*

• *"Being a parent means having to make sacrifices you might not want to make—you just make them anyway. If you're un-happy with this arrangement, you probably weren't ready to be a parent. Being there for my kids has always made me happy— I hope someday you'll understand what good things being a parent brings you, instead of only seeing what it's taking away from you."*

6. Pulling rank

Pulling rank is usually a last resort. It's the tactic used when all other tactics have failed. It's the ace in the hole that can be played at the end of a disagreement when no other ma-neuver has managed to persuade you to back down from your stance. It's often the only rationale available in instances where there really is no logical basis for a position. It's the manipulator's trump card, the equivalent of using, *"Just be-cause...,"* or, *"Because I said so,"* as a compelling reason for do-ing anything. Although transparent in its strategy and weak in any persuasive basis, it is surprisingly effective in delivering the knock-out punch in an argument because their basis in simple fact makes these statements difficult to dispute.

Examples of pulling rank
- "She's _my_ child!"
- "You're not her mother!"
- "You can't tell me what to do with my own son—he's not your child!"

That such statements are true often stops you dead in your tracks; after all, how can you argue with reality? When confronted with such statements, simply remember that the facts were never in question. No one is disputing whose child this is—you both clearly know which one of you is the parent. What should be in question is the illogical idea that being a child's biological parent counts for anything more than genetics.

Contrary to what the parent would have you believe, bringing a child into the world in itself does not entitle a parent to a built-in set of rights or privileges. This manipulation can work only if you buy into the premise that biology is an entitlement and that the act of *becoming* a parent carries equal or higher rank than that of *being* one.

Sample Responses
- "Of course she's your child—no one has ever questioned that. But what we're talking about here is who has primary responsibility for making these kinds of decisions for her."
- "Yes, I realize I'm not her mother. I didn't bring her into the world, but I seem to have inherited the responsibility of judging what is and is not good for her, for the time being."
- "I know that technically he's not my son, but as long as he's in my care, I'm in a better position to decide what I feel is best for him."

The two most important things to keep in mind in dealing with conflicts such as these are to stay calm and to keep an open mind. Never allow yourself to become part of the problem. By maintaining a calm and rational demeanor, you refuse to allow people to draw you into their manipulations, no matter which type they try.

You know as well as anyone that you will not always be right in any given situation, and you must remain willing to acknowledge when you have been in the wrong. But you must also resist the temptation to accept responsibility for more than your share merely in the interest of avoiding conflict or hard feelings. And remember that manipulations go both ways—be alert to them when others may be using them, but don't forget that you may be capable of putting them to use when the heat is on you.

Things Every Second-Time Parent Should Do

As you travel into the practical territory of raising a second family, please bear in mind that this chapter is not designed to be a resource directory to provide you with the valuable addresses and phone numbers you'll need for locating roadside assistance. The tools outlined here are offered as suggested courses of action and general guidelines to use as you begin to identify the kinds of help and support you'll need on the road and to get a bearing on the kinds of social, legal, financial, and emotional difficulties you're sure to encounter along the way.

So crucial is the need for outside support that a comprehensive resource directory has been compiled and can be found in the appendices at the end of this book. Use this chapter to narrow down the kinds of assistance you're looking for, and then refer to the appendices to find it. Each family will certainly have its own individual needs and will have to decide which steps and directions suit its particular situation. Each item in this chapter identifies a common-sense yet commonly overlooked course of action that could mean the difference between struggling in isolation with a silent burden or managing your lot with grace and dignity. This chapter will help you understand why outside support and services are so valuable. The appendices beginning on page 225 will help you figure out where to go to get them.

1. *Know your rights*

Your ability to cope with and survive the journey of parenting your grandchildren will be infinitely easier if you are an informed traveler. Those whose grandchildren have been placed with them by court order in a formal arrangement will have very different rights than those whose grandchildren were dropped off by parents who have neither given the grandparents a clear indication of their expectations nor any idea of how long this arrangement is anticipated to last. Likewise, will the grandparents' rights be very different if the parents remain in the home but have given unofficial control of raising their children to the grandparents. Whatever your case, it pays for you to be aware of the boundaries and limitations of your legal responsibility. In all cases, you need to know where the parents' rights end and where yours begin.

Many grandparents accept court placement of their grandchildren following reports of abuse or neglect made to police or social service agencies. The courts often prefer to place children in the care of grandparents or other relatives in lieu of foster care, for obvious reasons. Therefore, having the legal system involved can prove to be both an asset and a liability.

If the grandchildren have been removed from their parents' custody by legal intervention as a result of abuse, neglect, or having been born with drugs in their system, a force larger and more powerful than the family has already deemed the parent at least temporarily unsuitable. In families where the system is not involved, it may well be the informed opinion of the grandparents that the children's parents are unfit, but without legal intervention, this conclusion amounts to no more than a matter of opinion—and opinions, no matter how informed, carry no weight where the care and placement of children are concerned.

One clear advantage for grandparents who are involved in the system is that they are spared the ugly burden of having to prove that their children are unsuitable parents, as this determination has already been made by an outside party. If the law has already recognized or appointed the grandparents as a child's official caretaker, no amount of personal disagreement or ill feelings between family members will have the power to undo this decision. Having the law on their side gives these grandparents the power and leverage that other grandparents lack. The clear benefit of court involvement here is that it removes the struggle for care and control over the children from between parents and grandparents and places it in the hands of an outside third party.

Unless, of course, the family chooses to use the court's placement as a quiet means of outsmarting the system. Having children placed by court order with other family members gives many parents room to take their children back in without the approval or knowledge of the system. Of course, if this deception is to be successfully pulled off, the other family members must be willing to become part of the conspiracy. If you are a grandparent with a grandchild in your care by court order and a parent who is using the rationale, *"But who will know the difference?"* to cajole you into disobeying the order, beware. While many families get away with this deception, justifying it by believing that it benefits everyone (the child is back with the parent and the grandparents are spared the burden), other families do irreparable damage by taking such risks. As a grandparent, you may be faced with having to make some difficult choices and set some firm limits in order to avoid being drawn into such a scheme. The long-term price for defying such a court order far outweighs the short-term benefits of second-guessing the system and taking the law into your own hands. You could end up losing the kids altogether by participating in such a subterfuge.

But there are many drawbacks as well to having an objective and impartial system take responsibility for making such major decisions for you. The first is that the system itself is often too objective and too impartial. The difficulty for grandparents who are caught up in the labyrinth we call our legal system is that they lose control over all decision-making and many times have no say at all with regard to anything concerning the children. Ironically, when the fight stays at home between parents and grandparents, the grandparents wind up with more power of persuasion. When the law steps in, a cold and complex bureaucracy takes over the role of making decisions of lasting impact on the parents, grandparents, and grandchildren alike.

The system by nature has no compassion and lacks the ability to be sensitive to the unique and individual nature of each case. Under penalty of legal recourse, the family is forced to comply with its every decision when it comes to what role each member can or cannot play in the children's lives, regardless of whether these rulings seem unfair or unreasonable. While they may appear reasonable on paper, in practice legal rulings and stipulations may prove to be unrealistic and impractical. This is the very reason so many families conspire to disregard the mandates and do as they see fit.

If the court system is involved in your case, be an informed participant. Investigate the laws and policies affecting your particular situation. What are your rights and responsibilities with regard to the children? What are the parents'? What are the parents required to do or prohibited from doing? What are the terms and conditions governing parental visitation? Are visits to be supervised by an approved monitor? What are the consequences if the parents fail to meet their obligations? What are the consequences of your failure to report noncompliance on the parent's part? Is the arrangement permanent or temporary? Under what conditions can you petition to make a temporary situation permanent? Is the parent required to provide some financial support, or do you now qualify for foster parent status and benefits? All of these questions may seem basic and logical, but it is surprising how frequently they go unasked. Making assumptions around such vital issues has led many grandparents into troublesome situations because they realized that clarification was needed only after something went wrong. Don't be an after-the-fact advocate.

Gather as much detail as possible directly from the source. Don't rely on the parents to interpret for you the court's rulings or explain to you what's expected of you or of them. Get the names of any attorneys, judges, advocates, or social workers involved with the case and speak to them directly whenever and wherever possible. Don't allow the parents to keep you in the dark about the terms of any court orders or rulings that directly affect you—this leaves too much room for manipulation. If they object to your speaking directly to any party by using the plea, *"Don't you trust me?"* take this as a warning sign that something is not quite right. If you are all on the same team, working together toward what is ultimately in the best interest of the children, clarification is not an issue of trust, and there is no room for secrecy.

There are likewise benefits and drawbacks to having no system involvement in family matters. If there is no formal arrangement dictating your role as caregiver, negotiations (if any) are left for you and the parent to hammer out between yourselves. When it is strictly a family matter, you may not have the leverage with the parent that the legal system gives you, but in exchange you gain the flexibility of being able to make more individualized arrangements. The problem here, though, is that as a family member, you have no clout and cannot therefore force the parent to comply with any terms of any agreement you may have made with one another. Without a formal and legally binding contract with regard to the care of the children, you have no way of securing financial support from the parent or even establishing a consistent schedule of visits. Verbal agreements are easily broken, but many grandparents find that keeping the legal system out of their lives is worth the sacrifices.

If you are a grandparent with grandchildren at home and you have no formal arrangement to bind you, you'll find yourself with precious little in the way of built-in legal protection. Should you decide that legal action is your only recourse to get financial support, or if you feel that petitioning for custody or legal guardianship is your only way to secure that the parent won't undo everything you've done, you may find that the law most often favors the biological parent to the exclusion of the grandparent.

Gaining custody or legal guardianship often requires solid evidence that the parents are unfit or are willing to voluntarily forfeit their parental rights. Although keeping the children in the grandparents' care may realistically be the best alternative, the law continues to strive for "family reunification"—keeping the parents and children together at all cost. In this respect, anything that comes between parents and their children (including well-intentioned family members) is often viewed as a threat to the preferred outcome. Given that the law is biased in favor of parents, some grandparents have had their good intentions backfire on them and have been seen in the eyes of the law to be destructive influences, needlessly meddling in the lives of their children and grandchildren.

Whatever your case may be, your position will be strengthened if you have the forces of knowledge and information on your side. Do not let the child's unpredictable or unreliable parent dictate what you will or will not do on the child's behalf. Don't be afraid to consult with social workers or child advocates, even if the system is not involved, if only for the purpose of finding out what rights you have and what services are available to you and your family. Explore custody issues, including power of attorney, adoption, and legal guardianship or similar alternatives that may be options for you, even in cases where you are uncertain about how long the children will be in your care. Although these options offer more protection and give grandparents authority rather than informal consent to make decisions affecting their grandchildren, each carries with it its own set of benefits and drawbacks.

Speak to people who know and who can help you decide whether you need the law behind you in your case, or if you are better off leaving well enough alone. Seeking out information *before* you need it can make the difference between whether you'll end up in more of a proactive or a reactive position in your role as grandparent caregiver.

2. *Investigate financial and medical assistance*
In the spirit of being informed and checking out anything that might help to lighten your heavy load, financial and medical assistance should not be ruled out. It doesn't take superior intellect to understand that raising children costs money. Most grandchildren do not arrive at their grandparents' homes with a built-in budget or expense account included in their belongings. In reality, many arrive with little more than the clothes they're wearing, while others barely have those. Caught off guard, the vast majority of grandparents have not factored the cost of raising another family into their already tight budgets.

Immediate needs such as clothing, food, a spare set of sheets—and for infants, diapers, formula, cribs, and car seats—seem overwhelming enough. Then come the long-range considerations of school uniforms, school supplies, day care, toys, birthday parties, class trips, and sports equipment, not to mention the cost of shots, medical check-ups, eyeglasses, and braces. Where will the money come from? In most cases, it will *not* come from the parents. Although many parents do contribute, the bulk of unforeseen and day-to-day expenses that cannot be tallied up falls on the grandparents.

In order to meet the financial challenge, many grandparents are forced out of retirement and back into the work force to earn extra income. Other grandparents who work are forced to quit their jobs, unable to find or afford adequate child care. All in all, the financial toll on grandparents can be devastating.

Raising children, even under the best of conditions, is costly and takes tremendous skill and resourcefulness. Raising children with no preparation is nearly unimaginable. In spite of working their entire adult lives, many grandparents are barely able to support themselves; they exist only on the limited or fixed incomes provided by retirement or Social Security benefits. Perhaps you are one of those who has spent a lifetime saving for the luxury of living comfortably, only to find yourself once again pinching pennies and clipping coupons just to make ends meet. In one fell swoop, your peaceful retirement has been transformed into a vivid recreation of your struggles as a first-time parent.

There may be help for you if you look for it and are willing to accept it. If you are on a limited or fixed income, you may qualify for financial assistance through various government agencies. But if you're like most people, finding these resources will not be nearly as difficult as qualifying for them...that is, if you're even willing to humble yourself to go this route in the first place. Because of their pride, many people would rather go hungry than accept "welfare." But if this is the only resource standing between you and losing everything in order to support your new family, don't be too proud to accept what is rightfully yours.

Many government programs are designed specifically to help children in need. Of course, these benefits can be used or abused by their recipients. The fact that some people have taken advantage of such programs should not dissuade you from using them in the precise manner for which they were intended. The stigma attached to receiving public benefits is a grim reality; however, it may be worth running the risk of being stigmatized in order to have access to benefits that could allow you and your family to exist more comfortably—better to be humble than hungry!

Perhaps more importantly, such programs also offer medical coverage for children. In the event that the child's parents work or receive public assistance that carries its own medical insurance, this is a relief. But because of their parents' own instability, many grandchildren in the care of their grandparents have no medical coverage to protect them. For a grandparent, adding a grandchild to an existing medical plan is in most cases unprecedented, but it may be worth a phone call to inquire as it has been known to happen. Without medical coverage, a childhood accident or a bout with a typical childhood illness could devastate what little is left in your savings account.

Benefits like Medicaid can be an option. If your grandchild qualifies for Medicaid, it can relieve at least a portion of the worry and financial strain on you. If the child is disabled, he or she may qualify for Supplemental Security Income (SSI), and if the child's parents are deceased, he or she may qualify for Survivor's Benefits through Social Security. In addition, families of victims of violent crime may have various forms of support and assistance available to them through victim's rights organizations in their community. All of these are worth investigating. Consult the resource directory at the end of this book to get you started.

The point being made here is that, if you need it and are willing to accept it, there is probably help available to you somewhere. Having never been through this before, you are probably unaware of the agencies and services at your disposal. It may take some detective work to unearth the services you need, but don't give up. Call your local social service organizations, child welfare agencies, family counseling centers, hospitals, and clinics. Don't be afraid to call agencies in your community that serve children and older adults and ask questions. There are many people out there who make their life's work dealing with these kinds of problems, and they often hold the keys to unlocking just the resource you need.

Consult the state and federal government listings in your local phone directory for numbers to your public welfare and Social Security offices. Also look for the numbers to Legal Aid organizations, which provide free legal advice and assistance to those who qualify. And don't forget to get in touch with organizations serving senior citizens (if your age qualifies you for this status) for additional information and support. As more and more grandparents are faced with raising their grandchildren, these organizations are becoming more familiar with the questions and increasingly more ready with the answers you need. You're not alone, so there's no need for you to go it alone.

3. Find your voice

For your own survival as a grandparent raising grandchildren, as well as for the benefit of the countless others living this experience, do not forget that you have a strong and important voice. In the case of any disease, epidemic, or social ill, little attention is ever paid to a problem if the numbers affected are small and silent. If current trends continue, the number of grandparent-headed families is certain to increase. If all those who are affected remain silent about their struggles, it is likely that their need for services and assistance will be overlooked. Little time, energy, or funds will be expended to help those families in need if they fail to call attention to themselves, assert their needs, and exercise their rights.

Legislative, social, political, and policy changes are driven by need and demand. By speaking out and making their presence known, grandparents may unify to become a powerful voice whose largely unrecognized needs cannot so easily be ignored. Let's face it, the more organized and outspoken a group is (regardless of its size) the more urgent its need is deemed to be—and the more priority its demands are given. It is often through the efforts of the persistent few who refuse to go away that small but significant changes are made for all.

Grandparents raising grandchildren remain for the most part a hidden minority. They silently go about the business of managing the family's affairs and allow few others (with the exception of one another) to know of the extent of their struggles. Grandparent support groups are becoming more common and are a vital outlet for frustration as well as sources for valuable resources and well-needed information. But many grandparents remain reluctant to call attention to themselves and their situations, fearing that they'll be judged or misunderstood by others. They feel badly enough about the problems they're having without calling unwanted attention to them.

But don't allow your pride, shame, guilt, or embarrassment to prevent you from being recognized as a growing social force. Let those without family problems be the first to cast judgment on you. In the task you have taken on, there is nothing to be ashamed of—you didn't create the multitude of problems that brought your grandchildren to your door. And no matter what difficulties your adult child may have gotten tangled up in, they reflect only on your child as a separate individual with free choice and free will, not on you as a poor or inadequate parent.

Perhaps like many others, you've been taught and have adopted the philosophy that what happens inside your home is no one else's business. Or perhaps, *"What will the neighbors think?"* was one of the credos by which your own family lived." If either was the case for you, it will be terribly uncomfortable for you to begin opening the door to allow others to see inside your home, not to mention your heart.

Perhaps you blame yourself and therefore fear the same or an even worse judgment from others. Perhaps you are ashamed or embarrassed at having raised a child who is unable to care for another human being. Blaming yourself for the predicament you're in will only cause you to isolate yourself. And your isolation will make it even more difficult for you to reach out to others for assistance because you imagine they will confirm your worst fear that it's really your fault you have ended up in this predicament.

Keep in mind that others rarely judge us as harshly as we judge ourselves. More importantly, no individual has the right to judge us. Those who feel the need to pass judgment on others are often closed-minded individuals who choose to measure others by the very rigid and unrealistic standards they have set for themselves. Judgmental individuals are by nature intolerant, and the opinions of intolerant individuals should carry no weight and have no significance in our lives.

Why, then, do so many of us give these very same individuals so much power? If our fear of judgment leaves us struggling with our problems alone, we are in essence allowing those whose opinions are of little consequence to us to dictate our behavior and keep us from fully rising to the challenge. We've let the narrow-minded few become the cause of our own undoing.

Never allow the opinions of the few and the narrow-minded to keep you in isolation. The world contains just as many kind and caring people as it does critical and judgmental ones. Those who are critical of others are often more outspoken about their opinions and are thus more visible, but just because they're more conspicuous doesn't mean they're any larger in number. Because their voices are louder and their messages sharper is no reason to allow them to come between you and your need to connect with those whose voices are in harmony with yours. Perhaps a more effective philosophy would be, *"Never allow what you fear others will think to be the deciding factor for what you do."* We cannot afford to place the responsibility for our livelihood in the hands of the insensitive or intolerant few.

Speak up with dignity and conviction about your situation, your views, your difficulties, and your needs. It requires much more strength of character to face such challenges than it does to stand in judgment of them. Let those in the community as well as in the local, state, and federal government know you are out there. Doing so may not automatically secure broad social change or immediate recognition of your rights—and it may not even guarantee you the protection you need when you need it—but it's still worth the effort. We don't really know what will happen if we take action in our lives, but we certainly do know what will happen if we don't.

4. Get support

Life is difficult enough all on its own, but the difficulties weigh much more heavily on us if we carry our burdens alone. For grandparents, both peer and professional support can make the difference between coping with the pressures or crumbling under their weight. It's often much easier for grandparents to accept that the family disruptions will have a negative impact on their grandchildren and to vigorously seek support for them than it is for them to grant themselves the benefit of the same doubt. Many of us have been indoctrinated with the belief that, if we prove not to be invincible, this means we're weak. We are led to believe (or manage to convince ourselves) that if we ask for help with a task or problem, we reveal our stupidity. Therefore, we waste time and energy struggling endlessly to solve a problem we can't seem to beat, stubbornly refusing to ask for assistance for fear that we'll let others know how "incompetent" we really are.

Such attitudes, for the most part, seem to be rooted in our own overdeveloped egos rather than in reality itself. If we never allow ourselves to holler for help, it's highly unlikely that we'll stay sane under grueling life circumstances. We can make life much easier for ourselves if we understand that being aware of our limitations is in itself a strength and that refusing to face our limitations is the only true sign of weakness. It requires much more courage to accept that we need the help of others than it does to pretend that we're superhuman. Needing help and allowing others to give it takes strength because it requires us to put aside our fears and to trust. Trusting no one and putting on like we don't need anyone's help is no great act of courage.

Grandparents must be willing to take stock of their strengths, but they must also admit, however reluctantly, that they are not superhuman. Peer support from fellow grandparents can at times be the only lifeline linking people to the hope, encouragement, and strength they need just to get by. Fellow grandparents are the best sources of information because you can count on the fact that at least one of them has already run across the same questions that you are asking now—and they might have done some important research you could benefit from. There is no better research than life experience. The experiences of others provide us with indispensable information because they have already made our mistakes for us so we can avoid making them ourselves.

By isolating, you not only deprive yourself of valuable knowledge, support, and expertise, but you also deprive others of your wisdom. Support groups are a two-way street—they're about give as much as they are about take. Many people make the mistake of viewing support groups from the standpoint of, "*What can those people tell me?*" If you have bought into the misconception that you can do everything yourself, you will no doubt believe that you can survive perfectly well without someone else's input. And maybe you can. But this is only half of what support groups are about. If you aren't there, you may be withholding a very small but vital key that could unlock a world of information for another person. You can't possibly have lived through the difficulties you have without having gained some valuable knowledge, and you may have just the piece of information someone else is looking for. It's selfish for you to avoid support groups simply because you feel there's nothing there they can offer you. We shouldn't measure life in terms of what we can get, but rather by how much we have to give.

Counseling for children, family members, and yourself can help everyone learn to communicate more openly, to be more in tune with how the others feel, and offer more effective ways of working together as a team. All families are systems comprised of interacting parts. When one member of the system has a problem, the others are affected either by direct impact or by the indirect impact the problem has on the functioning of the system as a whole. Which member serves as the "identified problem" in any family system is irrelevant. Treating this individual alone is only marginally helpful if the system is not treated as a whole. Doing so is the equivalent of replacing the batteries in a watch but leaving the time set wrong. The watch may now run perfectly, but unless the time is reset, it's still useless as a timepiece.

Like the gears that drive the watch, each of us has learned to serve a specific role in the family's overall functioning. Be open to seeking counseling for yourself—you, too, are an integral gear in the family mechanism. You may not be able to fix the broken part by doing so, but you can impact the performance of the system as a whole by finding ways to work around it. Family members often assume the posture of, *"Why do I need help? I'm not the one with the problem. He is!"* Or, if the one member who is in obvious need of help refuses it, the others will groan, *"If she gets help, I'll go, too; otherwise, forget it. I'm not going to do anything unless she is willing to."* Be careful of these thoughts. Your stubbornness might cause you to throw out the baby with the bath water.

By drawing this kind of a line in the sand and asking the other person to cross it first, you place the health of the entire family in the hands of its most unhealthy member. Is this the person you really want calling the shots? Why should the growth and strength of the entire family rest on whether or not one member (typically the sickest member) is willing to seek help? Don't allow the health of the family as a whole to be determined by the strength of its weakest member. The watch will run only as efficiently as its damaged gear will permit, until that gear is either repaired or replaced. Since families are more complex than watches, the damaged parts are not so easily repaired or replaced. With help we are more likely to be able to work around them in some way. Building a bypass around the problem allows the family to continue to function in spite of the needed repair and, more importantly, keeps the impairment from holding back the smooth operation of the unit.

By being unwilling to seek help, the rest of the family gives the so-called "problem person" the message that he or she is still in control of the family. Once again, the actions of one member call the shots for the entire family. This member's refusal or resistance to change is given the power to hold the entire family hostage. On the other hand, moving on with your own growth allows the family to take back control by refusing to allow the problem person's resistance to drag the rest of the family down. In many respects, the action of the family in seeking help sends to the resistant member the definitive message, *"Catch up or be left behind!"* The choice is clear. Counseling and support may not fix the family problem, but they can help the stronger members keep their strength so they can continue to function in spite of the impairment.

5. *Keep accurate records*

Imagine that you have been contracted to do a job or perform a professional service for someone. There would be little doubt in your mind about the importance of keeping thorough and accurate records of your work. But when the services being provided involve family, and the task contracted is personal in nature instead of professional, the idea of keeping records takes on a very different tone. It just wouldn't seem right to keep a tally on a labor of love, now would it?

At the risk of sounding clinical or even crass, grandparents raising grandchildren (unless they have legally adopted the children) are literally providing a service for someone else—namely the parent. Regardless of the relationship between the grandparents and the parents, the need for keeping thorough records should not be underestimated. Don't find yourself in a situation where you wish you had taken note of a certain event or kept a receipt. It is far better to have too much extraneous information than to be without that one vital piece of information you either can't remember or can't find. This means keeping track not only of expenses incurred directly as a result of caring for your grandchildren, but also taking note of important events and agreements.

Here are some helpful hints:
* **Keep receipts**—Keep grocery receipts, rent receipts, mortgage and utility bills, along with any other records reflecting your income and expenditures. These will document the impact that the added family member(s) have had on your dwindling budget. Chart your general cost of living as well as costs directly related to your grandchildren's care. You not only need a record of what expenses

the children incur directly, but you'll also need to document the impact this change has made on your overall lifestyle.

• **Maintain a medical log**—Make note of the children's medical histories, hospitalizations, major illnesses, allergies, shots, immunizations, doctor's visits, medications, missed school days, etc., being certain to include any expenses incurred indirectly as a result of securing medical treatment for them. For example, if you've missed work days due to the children's illnesses or medical appointments, be sure to make note of this.

• **Develop contracts and agreements**—Take note of any requests you make for assistance from the child's parents, along with anything they have agreed to contribute. Be sure to include any articles or items they may have purchased for the family on behalf of the children as well as those purchased for the children specifically. Record any money they have contributed or have agreed to contribute. Whenever possible, spell out in writing any agreements made between yourself and the parents about what financial support they will provide. Document any agreements they have made with regard to the decisions you will be empowered to make on the child's behalf. Be sure to have any such written contracts signed by both parties and even notarized whenever appropriate. An argument will likely ensue at your suggestion that any such agreements be written and signed, but this should not discourage you from asking for their cooperation. Remember, this is business, it's not personal. If the parents deny your request, be sure to make a note of their refusal.

• **Keep a journal**—Maintain a grandparent's journal of significant events related to the children. Keep track of phone calls from the parents, contact between parents and children (noting who initiated the contact), letters, cards, gifts, visits that took place and their duration (if necessary, the children's state of mind at the end of such visits), and any visits that were promised but failed to take place. And most importantly, be fair. Don't meticulously record what the parents *didn't* do and overlook what they *did*.

Give credit where credit is due. You can bet that the parents are keeping a mental tally of what they've done—a tally that might be much more detailed than yours.

"How," you may ask, *"will I ever find the time to do all of this without hiring a private secretary?"* It will be difficult to find this time, especially on top of the added responsibility of being a parent again. But it is essential to establish a system whereby you have a written record of your services. It's always better to be prepared for what might never happen than to be unprepared for what actually occurs. Should you ever find yourself in the unfortunate position of pitting your word against the word of your adult children, you will be infinitely more credible if you have taken the time and the extra steps required to maintain a thorough account of your role as caregiver. But again, be fair in your account of the events. If you've only made a note of the bad things and the parent provides proof of having provided some real support that you've overlooked, your record-keeping could backfire. It could appear that you're involved in a personal vendetta against the parent, thus destroying any credibility you've worked so hard to establish.

Try not to feel that you're being distrustful or paranoid, and don't allow your adult child to make you feel guilty over your desire to establish documentation. Consider this the business aspect of your grandparenting role and remember that, in business, trust is not a factor and there's no room for guilt. You are in essence providing a generous service to any parent whose child is in your care. Like any wise service provider, you should document your expenses as proof of services rendered. These records may come in handy at some future point in substantiating your overall financial need, should you decide to apply for benefits of some kind. Further, just *knowing* that you're keeping records shows everyone that you're serious, and it can often be enough to deter the parent from playing games with you.

Many grandparents who feel uncomfortable viewing their role in such an impersonal manner have unknowingly left themselves open to being taken advantage of. Failure to keep track of expenses, agreements, emotional impact, broken promises, etc. makes it difficult to dispute the parents' verbal claim that they're doing their share and contributing to the overall well-being of the children. It's not beyond the scope of possibility for parents to disappear for extended periods with no contact, only to return and demand that the children be returned to their care. In the event that you decide to take on the formidable challenge of fighting this or other custody-related battles in a legal forum, your compiled evidence of the parents' failure to provide care may not serve as solid proof, but it will undoubtedly strengthen your case by showing you are not messing around when it comes to the children. This extra effort may well prove to be the factor that shows you are willing to go to any lengths to secure the safety and security of your grandchildren's home environment.

It has often been said that it is unwise either to trust everyone or to trust no one. As a grandparent, you may be inclined to feel too trusting of others (particularly family) and allow them to discourage you from taking an active stance in your role as caregiver. As the expression suggests, avoid approaching all such interactions with skepticism, spotting dishonesty and potential manipulation even when it isn't there. But likewise, don't be so naive that you forget that you're in the precarious position of protecting the interests of children who are not your own.

To gain important objectivity, it may help to ask yourself what you would do if the children in your care were not family members. If you were caring for your best friend's children or your neighbor's children, would you do things differently? Looking at it from this perspective can help you to remove the emotional connection that can blur and cloud the more practical issues.

Be a smart advocate grandparent. Act in the manner suggested by your rational mind, not that dictated by your sense of family loyalty or commitment alone.

$$8$$

Parenting Skills You Didn't Need the First Time

Much like your journey through parenthood, the road to becoming a parent again is a long and bumpy one. You will find that many of the tools you need to survive this new expedition are the same ones every parent needs. Having already raised one set of children, you have put together a valuable tool box that contains most of the basic equipment. Some of these tools may be a bit rusty, and you may consider others to be old and obsolete; but regardless of what make or model your existing equipment may be, each piece is still valuable in its own right. And it's quite true that older technology tends to be of more lasting quality, and often proves to be much sturdier, than the newest technologies. The parenting skills you learned the first time are still with you. Dust them off—you'll need them all!

But there are some skills you will need as a grandparent that you didn't need when raising your own children. These new skills arise from your change in course—you've never been down this road before, and the hazards of the new route you're traveling probably won't reveal themselves to you until you've stumbled directly into them.

For example, you're in a position now where you have to explain your family situation to others because it's out of the ordinary, whereas your own family situation probably didn't raise any eyebrows because it was no different from the rest. But the rules have changed—you're a parent right enough, but it's different when the children you're raising are not your own.

The following items will help you to identify and understand the differences between being a first- and a second-time parent. They are designed to provide you with some direction when the weathered parenting road map you're using doesn't quite match your present surroundings.

Dealing with Those Difficult Questions

It's a fact of life that when something is out of the ordinary, it arouses curiosity. As a grandparent raising a grandchild, you'll need to become comfortable with the idea of being asked questions and be ready with answers regarding your family situation. If you have not already, you will be the target of inquiries ranging from the sincere concern of professionals who are directly involved with your family to the curious and often insensitive probing of casual acquaintances. Through it all, please remember two important things: (1) *you do not owe the entire world an explanation for your situation simply because it's out of the ordinary;* and (2) *not all of those who ask about your circumstances have a genuine need to know.* It will be up to you to judge on an individual basis, from person to person and from situation to situation, how much you will say and to whom you will say it.

Be sure in all cases to avoid the evils of extremes. An *all or nothing* approach will either lead you to offer the complete and unabbreviated version of your story to any sympathetic ear or cause you to keep it all under your hat with the thought that no one has the time or interest to hear your sad tale. Somewhere between these two extremes you will find the right level of disclosure to fit the situation. For example, teachers, school counselors, nurses, day care workers, social workers, and other professionals directly involved with family care play different roles and have very different reasons for their inquiries than will your neighbor, mail carrier, or hairdresser. With some professionals, the whole, unedited version is indicated, whereas with others, like teachers and medical professionals, the rules are not so clear. Although technically these individuals are involved with your family, their involvement is often indirect.

With service providers and other concerned individuals, a few general rules of thumb may help you narrow down the field of how much of your long and complicated saga to relate when questions arise. Although they may seem to be based on common sense, you'll be surprised by how quickly common sense can desert you when you're on the spot and overwhelmed by too many decisions and too much information.

When faced with personal questions, take into consideration the following:

1. *Who* is asking the questions?

What service or function are they providing? What is the minimum amount of information they need to have to adequately provide this service?

2. *Why* are they asking?

Given the circumstance, is their specific question a matter of simple curiosity or a request for a needed piece of information to serve a specific purpose? Remember, professionals can be nosy, too.

3. *What* information are they *really* looking for?

General, open-ended questions are often too broad and cause you to over-explain. Don't be afraid to ask for clarification before giving too much detail.

For example, when a doctor inquires, *"Where are Johnny's mother and father?"* this is an extremely general question. Taking into consideration the *"who"* and the *"why,"* you may need the doctor's help in narrowing down the *"what."* Is the doctor seeking medical history, trying to determine who to consult regarding treatment, or is the question simply designed to make conversation? Don't try to figure it out on your own. There is no need to relate the entire story from beginning to end for fear of missing the sought-after detail. It is never inappropriate to politely clarify by asking, *"What is it specifically you need to know?"*

In cases where someone's need to know is unclear or borne by interest rather than necessity, no one is a better judge than you of what is appropriate or what you feel comfortable discussing. You'll need to rely on your gut feeling to tell you the difference between concern and plain old curiosity. In dealing with the curious, there are polite ways to let them know that they've overstepped the bounds of your privacy. Never compromise yourself by being impolite in return, no matter how insensitive someone's comments or questions might be. Avoid instinctive retorts such as, *"It's none of your business."* While this may very well be the case, we can deliver the same message courteously with a simple reply like, *"My personal life really shouldn't concern you,"* or even by using some humor: *"There really isn't enough time in the world to explain the whole story."* The end result will be the same—you've gently and politely given the person the message to back off.

Whether we're dealing with questions, curiosity, or offhanded remarks, it's our job to always show more class than those who have been insensitive toward us. Remarks like, *"It's none of your business,"* are in themselves insensitive, not to mention hostile and defensive. And we all know what happens when we get defensive—we just arouse more curiosity because it looks like we've got something to hide. Being rude to intrusive people lowers us to their level and, personally, I recommend that we don't compromise ourselves in this way. By remaining dignified and courteous no matter the situation, we refuse to stoop to the level of others, and force them to rise to ours.

Difficult questions posed by outsiders are just a predictable part of the package for second-time parents. But perhaps the most difficult questions of all for grandparents to answer will be those that don't come from outsiders but from the grandchildren themselves. As the children grow older and are exposed to a wider variety of family environments, the complexity of these questions will increase. Some strategies for fielding basic questions are outlined in Chapter 4. (See the section on the unreliable parent and how much of the parent's problems a child needs to know.) But these general questions aside, your grandchildren will inevitably begin to pose such mind-boggling and seemingly unanswerable questions as, *"Why can't our family be more like Johnny's or Mary's?"*

In responding to such jaw-droppers, it will help you to keep in mind that, although they are as important as requests for specific information, these questions are really rhetorical. In other words, they're just statements posed in the form of questions. From your grandchild's point of view, these questions are more of an opportunity to make a point or express a feeling than they are to gather information. Because they come at you as questions, they may put you on the spot, making you feel you have to come up with an acceptable answer. They may even at times push a button and put you on the defense because of their provocative nature.

As a parent, you've probably learned that not every question needs an answer, and that some questions can be satisfied with a simple response. Resist your impulse to over-explain in an attempt to quiet your grandchildren's fears and relieve all of their doubts. In posing such questions, they are never in search of a detailed family history that identifies the cast of characters and explains how they all ended up where they are. Giving them detailed factual information may make you feel like you've answered the question to the best of your ability, but it will never satisfy the children's real need. Remember, they're not really looking for information in the first place; they're searching for something much greater.

The best way to figure out how to respond to such thought-provoking questions is to first listen carefully for what feeling or message the children are really trying to convey. When you've got it, simply reflect it back to them. By doing this, you're in essence teaching them the fine art of expressing their feelings. These questions are usually elementary attempts to tell you something they don't yet have the words to say.

Example #1:

A child asks: *"Grandma, why can't our family be normal, like Mary's?"*

The grandparent's natural reaction is to answer the question. The grandparent responds with: *"Our family is different from Mary's, and you know that. You need to stop worrying about what everyone else has and appreciate what you've got."*

Although the message the grandparent is conveying is perfectly valid, it has missed what the child was really trying to say.

Let's try it again:

Child: *"Grandma, why can't our family be normal like Mary's?"*

The real feeling or message is: *"I don't like being different."*

The grandparent responds: *"It's hard for you to feel different from the other kids, isn't it? Tell me what Mary's family has that makes you feel this way."*

By listening to what the child was really saying, the grandparent opened the door for the child to talk about the feeling of being different.

Example #2:

Child: *"Why can't I just go live with Mary? Her parents are neat."*

Feeling insulted, the grandparent's impulse is to reply: *"You think Mary's family is so neat. You'd be begging me to come get you! Everybody always thinks that other people have something better than they do. We always think the grass is greener on the other side of the street."*

Once again, the message is perfectly valid, but the child's point has been missed because of the grandparent's need to address the child's original question.

Let's try it again:

Child: *"Why can't I just go live with Mary? Her parents are neat."*

The real message is: *"Something is missing in our family that Mary's has."*

The grandparent responds: *"Seeing families like Mary's must remind you that something is missing here. Does that make you sad?"*

As you can see, no amount of factual information could satisfy these questions, because they're really messages in disguise. By resisting the impulse to explain or defend yourself in response, such questions become doorways to open dialog about what the children are thinking and how they're feeling. Don't miss such opportunities by being distracted by the question itself or by reacting to the internal buttons these questions can push. Listen to the feelings the children are trying to express and then give them the words to express them.

No amount of data or intellectual understanding could suffi-
ciently compensate for what they feel they are missing. Save
yourself the stress.

In addition to the questions others will ask of you and
those your grandchildren will ask of you, you will need to help
your grandchildren tackle questions asked of them by others,
particularly their peers. The only guarantee with such questions is that you should expect them and you should be prepared for them. Discuss this with your grandchildren *before*
their friends begin to ask where their parents are and why they
live with grandma and grandpa. The other kids are bound to
want to know at some point or another—discussions at school
about parents are a part of life and can prove uncomfortable
or even embarrassing if they catch your grandchildren off
guard. Preparation gives them time to get ready for the topic
when it arises rather than steering clear of such discussions
when they come up. Preparation can also keep them from
feeling they have to make up a story on the spur of the moment that might eventually come back to haunt them.

Please be clear when you're helping your grandchildren
prepare their responses that there is a difference between dishonesty and privacy. Be sure to ask your grandchildren for
their input about how much they can comfortably disclose to
their friends. And most importantly, help them to understand
that withholding information that's of no concern to others is
not being dishonest, but rather, it's respecting our individual
right not to broadcast our private affairs to all of society.
Having an unusual family circumstance or living in a nontraditional arrangement doesn't automatically grant the world unrestricted access to your personal business, nor does it oblige
you to offer anyone explanations about why your situation is
different from the rest.

Help your grandchildren learn to explain why they live
with grandma and grandpa without being secretive, apolo-
getic, or overly dramatic. Use creativity where appropriate,
but avoid the deadly, *"My daddy is an astronaut on a secret
mission,"* approach (unless, of course, this is the case). *"My
mommy is sick and can't take care of me,"* is often honest enough
to satisfy the curiosity of others without offering too much un-

necessary detail. The exact nature of the illness is really no one's business unless you decide otherwise.

Becoming a Stand-in, Not a Substitute Parent

No matter how convincingly you play the role of parent, there will be times when everyone is reminded that you are just holding a place in your grandchildren's lives. The gap separating you from your grandchildren is a constant reminder, making it hard to ignore that there is a parent missing in the space between you. Grandchildren adjust to being parented by their grandparents, but let's face it, they rarely play make-believe that their grandparents are really their parents. Although these children may seem very comfortable in their grandparents' care, they never lose sight of the fact that there is a generation missing in between.

For the children, the most painful reminders of how they are different from their peers will typically come during important special events such as parent/teacher conferences and parent/child activities at school. Although no one else may even notice the presence of the grandparent stand-in (many children's parents are older these days), the children will often feel that all eyes are on them. Being "different" in the slightest way is a curse for young people, who see fitting in with their peer group as a matter of life and death.

If your grandchildren are embarrassed to have you stand in, don't take their embarrassment personally. The fact that they are fortunate to have someone fill in for their parents when so many other children have no one at all is not the issue here. These events are glaring reminders to children of what they are missing out on. Take their embarrassment as a healthy reaction to being different. It's more about what they're lacking than it is about what they've gotten instead.

For these very reasons, some children fear these activities and try to avoid them altogether. Family night at school can be a dreaded arena of comparison in which children size up their families against the others and always seem to come up short. It would be understandable for children to shy away from taking part in an activity where they feel they can't compete.

Encourage them, but do not force them to confront this reality. Reassure them that the events themselves are not nearly as bad as the apprehension they create. In reality, the events we dread the most turn out to be more difficult than we had hoped but rarely as terrible as we had imagined. The fear of standing out can easily overpower their desire to participate in many of the rites of childhood. Our fears can either motivate us or paralyze us, depending on how we handle them. Help your grandchildren decide for themselves which approach is wiser. Gently steer them toward understanding that fear is temporary and passes as quickly as the circumstance that caused it, but missing a milestone event in their lives is a permanent and preventable loss.

It's difficult to understand why some children shy away from inviting friends over in order to avoid the inevitable and uncomfortable questions this brings up, while other children seem completely unscathed by their differences. Each child will perceive the same event in a unique and individual way. It's important that you remain sensitive to your grandchildren's individual impressions of how they measure up against their peers. Don't close them down by interpreting their sensitivity and embarrassment as personal rejection.

Childhood is filled with its own share of doubts and fears about whether or not we'll be accepted by others. How fiercely your grandchildren struggle with this issue is not a reflection of how well you are doing as a stand-in parent. Don't be afraid to commiserate with them about how awkward it is to be different, but also don't forget to reassure them that this difference makes them no less special in their own right. It's our differences, not our similarities, that in the end make us all unique and interesting.

Facing the Pressures of Special Occasions

Face it, there is no special aisle at your local greeting card shop for nontraditional families. Holidays and other special occasions, more than any other time, will bring us face to face with the realization that our family circumstance is not the stuff of greeting card sentiments. Tradition is mercilessly insensitive to changing times and the pressures faced by today's families. How do you buy a Mother's Day card for a mother who has been negligent? Should you even bother? How do you celebrate Christmas or Hanukkah with a parent in prison? Do you invite your drug-addicted son or daughter to your grandson's birthday party? Unfortunately, there are no simple or standard answers to questions the likes of these, and there is certainly no special chapter in the latest book of social etiquette you can use as a reference.

The dilemmas faced by those grandchildren who are brought up in the care of grandparents will become increasingly more complex as they grow older. They will experience quandaries such as, *"Do I get Mother's Day and Father's Day cards for my grandparents?" "Am I expected to?" "Do I treat my grandparents as if they were my mother and father?" "If I do, will this hurt my parents' feelings?" "If I recognize my mother and father, and not my grandparents, on Mother's Day and Father's Day, will I hurt my grandparents' feelings?" "Or , do I recognize both and act as if I have two sets of parents?"* As with the previous questions, there are no existing guidelines for dealing with such unique conflicts. Holidays and special occasions create enough problems for the average family, but they can send the rest of us into a moral, ethical, and emotional tailspin!

Greeting card companies seem to have conspired to make our lives much too complicated. As an unconventional family, you have the dubious luxury of starting from scratch when it comes to writing your own rules or creating your own traditions. You are in new territory where no book on social graces has dared to venture to light your way. The standard hasn't been set with regard to sending cards or buying holiday gifts for family members you've had a love-hate relationship with. Do you buy cards and gifts just because it's what you're supposed to do? And how can you pick out a card with a soppy sentiment when it seems so insincere? How do you face holiday gatherings and join in the spirit of celebration when you have such a heavy heart? Do customs count more than your feelings or principles? Should they?

The only guideline that might be able to help you to answer any or all of these questions is the simple rule, *"Do that which you will not regret."* This means doing what you think is right and not necessarily what seems to be most comfortable. Sometimes this will mean putting your own resentments and personal differences on the shelf in the interest of simply doing the right thing for the children. At other times it will mean leaving well enough alone in the interest of guarding them against further hurt. But no matter what, you are only human. You'll never be able to please everyone. You have neither the ability nor the responsibility to ensure everyone's happiness, so don't even try. Stay focused on what's right and not what you think will keep the peace or make the fewest waves.

"Do that which you will not regret," also means not allowing your own hurt, resentments, anger, or disappointments to guide you in making these kinds of decisions. If you fail to extend a kindness or invitation to the child's parent or another family member as a punishment for having disappointed you in some way, this will only make you guilty of causing the child to suffer for the parent's misdeeds. This is petty and self-righteous. You will regret it. On the other hand, if you go overboard with insincere generosity, you will feel phony and manipulative. You should. You will regret this as well. None of us is either all good or all bad—this principle applies as much to our family as it does to us. It is entirely possible for us to extend kind and heartfelt sentiments to someone with whom we have bitterly disagreed if we realize that the negatives in each person do not cancel out the positives. There are redeeming qualities in every person...some are just more of a challenge to find.

Your adult child is a package deal, as we all are as individuals—strengths and weaknesses all rolled into one. We can appreciate any person's strengths and enjoy an individual's positive qualities if we don't allow ourselves to be influenced by our tendency to dwell on human flaws. Would we toss out the heirloom vase because of its cracks, or do we accept the flaws as part of its character and history? Do the chips detract from the beauty of the piece or add to its depth? With people, we seem to have greater difficulty accepting the complete package, particularly when we're in conflict over their choices or lifestyles. But we can accept people without having to be in harmony with those aspects we can't overlook. Accepting them doesn't mean we're in agreement with behaviors or traits we strongly object to; it simply means we allow the positives and negatives to peacefully coexist.

Sometimes the best gift we can give to someone we love is our forgiveness for not being as we had hoped and our acceptance of being just as they are. We would certainly hope for the same courtesy ourselves, wouldn't we? Holidays and special occasions can bring out the best or the worst in us. They can expose us as petty, grudge-keeping, revenge-seeking cowards or they can offer us an opportunity to find the courage to put our differences aside and treat others with the same dignity and respect we'd ask of them.

Straddling the Generation Gap...x 2

There are few givens in the realm of raising children, but one thing is for certain—there will be a generation gap between all parents and their children. It's nearly a tradition for parents to squabble with their kids over clothing and hairstyles and for each generation to listen with equal disdain to the others' musical preferences. Certainly you can recall clashing with your own parents, just as you did with your children. You can guarantee the same pattern will repeat itself with your grandchildren—only with double the volume. There are two generations dividing you now, instead of just one.

If your own children thought of you as "out of it" or "old-fashioned," you can bet that to your grandchildren you'll seem nearly prehistoric. No offense, but a lot of time has passed since you were their age, and changes in trends and lifestyle are swift and unforgiving. Nevertheless, you have somehow managed to muddle through this clash of generations with your own children, as your parents did with you. You may be weary, but you'll have to find the strength to weather the storm again. And remember, unlike the case with your own children, you won't be able to measure the likes of your grandchildren by your own standards of taste and preference. The best way to judge whether their interests are on target and not off the scale of reason—given our changing times—is experience with other children in their age group.

Don't be afraid to talk to the parents of your grandchildren's friends to see if it is indeed the case when you hear that all too familiar wail, *"But everyone else is doing it!"* But do remember that, in keeping with tradition, just because everyone else is doing it doesn't necessarily make it the right thing for your family. You can count on your grandchildren to try to use the fact that you're older and behind the times to manipulate you into believing that if you weren't so out of touch, you'd be able to see things their way. Don't fall for this. Your principles still count, even when tastes and trends are in conflict.

You as the parent figure are the final judge and jury regarding what is acceptable or unacceptable within the bounds of your home. You should, however, not be above compromise if your ideals and standards with regard to music, styles of dress, etc. are a bit out of date. After all, you are two generations removed from your grandchildren. But bear in mind that compromise goes both ways—you don't always have to bow to accommodate your grandchildren's wishes, nor would it be fair in all cases for you to expect them to completely bend to yours. Together, you'll have to find an acceptable midpoint where each of you gives way a bit to the others' side. Negotiation gives children of all ages a sense of personal responsibility and shows them that you are fair and willing to be flexible. It can make them feel that all-important feeling that their views are meaningful, even though they won't always be honored. Being heard is often more valuable than getting your way. You don't have to like the other person's preferences to arrive at a place that's acceptable to both of you. With children and parents, the key seems to be in arriving not so much at what makes them both happy, but in determining what each can live with.

There are likewise some things that should not be open to negotiation, no matter how many generations separate you from your grandchildren. While matters of taste are subjective and compromising on them has no significant impact on a child's life, matters of safety and responsibility prove to be dangerous areas if their doors are left too far open for negotiation. These areas require clear and firm limits to be set by an authority figure. Here, it is your responsibility to remain in the driver's seat. You're in charge. You should not give the steering wheel to someone who has not yet learned to drive.

If you have house rules about chores, respect, conduct, drug use, violent behavior, dating, courtesy, etc., stand by them. Tastes and preferences have no place when values, morals, and principles are on the line. Old-fashioned or not, rules are rules, and you have the responsibility to set them and keep them. Don't feel that your rules must be behind the times because you're raising your grandchildren. Too many grandparents let their grandchildren set their own rules to avoid the stress of the children getting angry and reminding them that they're not their parents. Grandchildren or not, this is still a case of the students running the school.

It is inevitable that you will be accused of being old-fashioned. Expect this, get used to it, and even accept it as a compliment—it may be the only solid evidence you'll get that you're on the right track! Your grandchildren will be sharp enough to sense that your age difference and your role as stand-in parent are sensitive areas for you. They may try to use these as button pushers to get you to question yourself and your motives. Don't be fooled by their tactics. They may claim that your expectations of them are too rigid or unfair, forcing them to call upon those hair-raising battle cries of, *"But no one else has to...,"* or, *"If you trusted me, you'd let me...,"* when you insist on meeting their friends or expect a phone call to be advised of a change of plans. And you may even be tempted to give in on the grounds that perhaps times *have* changed and that maybe, just maybe, you are being unreasonable. When in doubt, check it out.

Checking with other parents can be helpful to either confirm or deny your grandchildren's claims that you are not with the times. But checking with others can also lead you to two very different conclusions. By checking with other parents and finding them much more lenient than you are, you may discover that the other parents are so wrapped up in their own personal or career endeavors that their lack of availability is being interpreted by their children as trust or flexibility. In this case, you'll be reassured that your seemingly stringent expectations are more on target than their permissive ones. Or, you might find that some of your expectations are driven more by your own overprotectiveness than by real necessity. Speak to others, but ultimately reserve the right to judge for yourself what approach fits best for you and your family.

Setting and Maintaining Firm Limits

Grandchildren who come to live with their grandparents often arrive with more than the average share of emotional and behavioral problems. Many have come from parents who were either permissive to the point of neglect or rigid to the extreme of abuse. The difficult task awaiting grandparents who are on the receiving end of either legacy lies in gathering together the scattered pieces of their grandchildren's lives and weaving those pieces into something whole and durable. Children need limits to make them feel safe. Grandchildren who come to live with their grandparents need to be introduced to healthy limits before they can hope to begin to understand the need for them, accept them, and eventually depend on them.

No matter how unhealthy, inconsistent, or nonexistent the parents' limits may have been, it is nonetheless disruptive for children to be shifted to a new environment in which the rules have suddenly and dramatically changed. You can expect that as they explore and experience the boundaries of their new environment, they'll be a bit skeptical. These grandchildren will need some time to test these new rules for consistency and fairness before being able to trust and accept the new deal.

Any transition involving a sudden shift in roles, rules, boundaries, expectations, or limits will set off a period of adjustment for everyone who's on the receiving end of this change. You can see this wave of adjustments in play even in situations as commonplace as a new boss arriving in the workplace. The employees who greet the new boss will meet the change initially with healthy skepticism until they've had a chance to test, challenge, and defy the new authority figure to see if she or he will be fair. This is the only way for others to decide whether to accept or reject their new leader. The job of captain of the ship is too important to trust to just anyone.

Transitions like these will set in motion a predictable sequence of stages for readjustment. Families go through them as well. Transitions and readjustments will follow not only when grandchildren come to stay, but also after any major change in family dynamics such as the following:

- divorce/separation
- remarriage
- when adoptive or foster children join an existing family
- when stepchildren and a step-parent join an existing family
- when a chemically dependent family member finds recovery
- when a codependent family member gets help and the chemically dependent member continues to drink or use
- when an absent or permissive parent decides to *"toughen up"*
- when a passive person begins to act assertively

Not only children, but anyone who experiences such shifts in a family's way of operating will be thrown off balance as the waves of change reach each individual and affect the way the system functions as a whole. The following is a brief description of five of the most predictable phases of adjustment that result from such major changes. Like the stages of the grieving process, these phases of transition may vary from individual to individual and from one situation to another. But what you can count on is that your grandchildren will probably greet their new surroundings and your new rules and expectations by playing out any or all of these stages:

1. Suspicion/speculation: A change has just taken place. This is the "feeling out" period during which the change is met with cautious skepticism. Will the change be temporary or permanent? Rigid or flexible? Fair or unfair? A newfound conviction or a passing fancy? Those witnessing the change will stay on the sidelines and watch from a safe distance.

They're looking for the motives behind the change. Is there a hidden agenda? When the change involves a new boss in the workplace, the employees will feed that boss with a long-handled spoon. In a family, the members witnessing the change will poke fun at it, or nervously make light of it. Your grandchildren, when they first arrive in their new environment, may seem distant, withdrawn, and standoffish. They're afraid to get too comfortable in case the change doesn't last.

2. *Resistance:* Family members, (or others, depending on the situation) begin to challenge the new arrangement. The authority figure who has either changed the rules or who has just taken over will be tested. Is he or she really serious about the change? Challenging the rules gives everyone an opportunity to see what (if any) consequences result if they fail to go along with the new order. This is their chance to resist before beginning to test it in earnest. In essence, they're digging in their heels at this stage and refusing to go along for the ride.

3. *Testing:* This is the point at which others (particularly children) begin to act out. They will disobey the new rules and may even disobey the same rule repeatedly. This reflects their conscious or unconscious desire either to force the person responsible for the change back into old behavior, or to simply scare the new person away. This testing demonstrates everyone's desire to regain the comfort or predictability they've lost in the transition.

With grandchildren, statements such as, "*My mom and dad would never do that,*" or, "*Mom and dad would always let me...,*" are indicators that what they once knew is now gone. Continuing to push against the same boundary or defy the same rule over and over again gives children in particular a chance to answer three important questions: *What are the consequences of disobedience? Will these consequences be equally, consistently, and fairly enforced?* and, *Are there loopholes in the new system?* There may be a brief period of cooperation during which it appears as if everyone has successfully adjusted to the change. . . but this is just the calm before the storm.

4. *Escalation:* This is the storm. If the limits and consequences have held up through the testing period and the parent or authority figure has failed to weaken, give in, or run

away, the intensity of the rebellion will increase. If other tactics have failed to shake the person's resolve, then sheer force or fatigue might just do the trick. This is the stage at which small children will have temper tantrums and adults may become pushy, threatening, or simply irritating in hopes that the authority figure will give in, if for no other reason than to shut them up. The person responsible for the change is most at risk of backing down at this stage, mainly from fatigue or sheer frustration.

5. Acquiescence: All attempts to stop the change have failed. The new rules have proven solid and unwavering, and the new arrangement is here to stay. The energy and efforts that had been devoted to resisting the change have all backfired, wearing down those who were resisting. The person at the helm of the transition has won this round (at least for the time being). There will be future rebellions, but they won't be as intense and they won't last as long.

Keep in mind that these stages are a sequential process, playing out in varying ways over differing periods of time. Becoming familiar with them will enable you to watch for them, prepare for them, identify them when they occur, and understand them in their proper context.

You must also understand that acquiescence will *not* occur if you give in or change your position in response to the resistance you're up against during any of these stages. You must remain firm and unwavering in your stance, staying calm, rational, and consistent in the face of the resistance, even when you feel like throwing your hands up in defeat. Giving in will only reinforce whatever behavior succeeded in causing you to give in. Giving in tells the other party (in this case, your grandchildren) that pushing you hard enough and long enough is well worth the effort because you'll eventually wear down and give them what they want. Giving in moves you both back to square one and assures that the next time you move through these stages, the rebellion you'll be up against will be more intense and the transition period will drag on even longer. Backing down teaches the other parties that your position is not solid and that it can be changed if the right kind and amount of pressure is applied.

The following is a narrative that illustrates how these stages play out in a real-life situation.

Annie

Annie, a single mother who has been overly lax with her children because of her excessive drinking, enters a treatment program. Newly sober and revitalized, she is ready to take matters back into her own hands. This commitment includes pulling in the reigns on her three teenage children, who have taken advantage of the intoxicated fog she's been in and have been doing exactly as they please.

The change: *Annie calls a family meeting and introduces a list of house rules, including assigned chores and a curfew of 10 P.M. The children are surprised and a bit put off at the idea of all of a sudden having restrictions put on their freedom.*

Phase 1. Suspicion/speculation: *The children greet their mother's plan with a jaundiced eye because they've been through her flights into health before. Knowing that all of her previous efforts to maintain family order were very short-lived, the kids mumble under their breath such things as, "Oh, here we go again," and, "We've heard this one before." The kids belittle Annie's efforts and refuse to take her seriously. If she were to back down because of their rolling eyes or mockery at this point, she would make it much harder on herself the next time she tried to reign them in. This is where she's made her mistake in the past.*

Phase 2. Resistance: *In the first few weeks after the family meeting, the chores are done haphazardly, if at all, and the curfew is completely ignored. The kids seem to be checking things out to see what mom will do if they just don't listen. So when Annie calls them on their disobedience, they get angry. After all, who does she think she is, changing the rules on them? Hoping that her persistence is nothing more than a passing phase, they continue to challenge her to see if she has the guts to punish them. When Annie flatly refuses to give in and even goes so far as to impose consequences for breaking the rules, the kids become angrier and are even more determined to keep the upper hand.*

Phase 3. Testing: *Now not only do the kids refuse to obey the rules, they refuse to accept the consequences, making life even more* *difficult for their weary mother. They seem to be saying, "That'll teach her to change the rules on us." If her new rules really are a passing phase, she's sure to have a change of heart when she sees how miserable the kids can become when they feel they're losing control. If Annie were to give in now, she'd only be teaching her kids that she's willing to take only so much of their antics before she gives up in despair. They would learn that they'd never really lost control and that bullying her will eventually cause her to back down.*

When Annie doesn't back down and even rises to the challenge, the power struggle between her and her kids is in full swing. Annie remains consistent and unwavering in her position, and it begins to take a lot more effort for her kids to argue with her than it does to just do what she asks. Out of sheer frustration, the children begin to do the chores, but only half-heartedly and with dramatic displays of what a terrible inconvenience they feel their mother is forcing them to suffer. They start to come home at 9:55 or at 10:10, and they never miss a chance to let their mother know how unbelievably unfair it is for them to be expected to come home so early. They go through periods of obeying the rules, only to later disobey the very same rules they had begun to obey. They're just letting Annie know that their compliance doesn't mean they've accepted her new regime...and they're just checking to see if she is still paying attention. They seem to be wondering if their mother will reward them for behaving by overlooking the odd slip-ups. At this point Annie reaches a critical crossroad. Now that the kids have shown some cooperation, she risks losing their respect altogether if her consequences for the odd slip-ups are too harsh. Remember, the kids are now looking for reasons to accuse her of being unreasonable so that they can continue to rebel. If they find no reward in obeying, Annie is in danger of losing what little cooperation she has managed to get. Much to their surprise, Annie recognizes their efforts, gives them credit for cooperating, and even cuts them some slack. But through it all she continues to demonstrate that there are still expectations and consequences in effect.

Phase 4. Escalation: *Annie has still refused to waver. The kids begin to panic for real. If this keeps up, they'll lose their freedom and will have to give up their control. It's time to pull out all the stops. This is the phase that could really drive her to drink. Unable* to find a weakness in her system, they try another approach. The rules and consequences themselves can't seem to be budged, so they begin to challenge the logic behind them. They engage in lengthy battles of wits with their mother, arguing over why they have to suddenly listen to her when she hasn't cared for so long. With their best mental manipulations, they try to poke holes in her reasoning, pointing out to her where she has messed up and how unfair it is for her to hold them to a higher standard than she has had to uphold. They next try guilt, reminding Annie of the many things she's failed to do as a mother, of the many hurts she's inflicted on them, and how she now has no right to take away the independence she had forced upon them. They even go so far as to accuse the program she is in of brainwashing her because everything was fine for them until she started talking to those counselors.

If Annie engages her kids in these battles of logic or falls into the trap of trying to explain or justify her actions to them, she essentially tells them that she's having trouble justifying them herself and will probably cave in if the right argument is found. In hopes that this doubt is lingering in their mother somewhere, the kids begin to look for it with a vengeance. Their disobedience escalates to dramatic proportions, making life even more miserable for their determined mother. In a last-ditch effort to wear her down, the theme becomes, "You just can't make me...no matter what." Giving in to such pressure is tempting and would certainly provide Annie with a welcome relief from the stress. Tired of fighting the endless battles, she even begins to feel that perhaps her kids are right—maybe she should just go back to the way things were. After all, she is really to blame for this mess.

Phase 5. Acquiescence: But at the urging of her counselor, Annie decides to hang tough. The rebellion goes on, but she continues to handle it without faltering. She listens tirelessly to their hurt, their anger, and their guilt-inducing attacks but refuses to back down. "Because I'm the parent and you're the child," becomes her catch phrase. If after everything they've tried she's still stood her ground, even her kids begin to believe that Annie must be serious this time. Conceding that she is at last back in charge, they decide that if they have any hopes of getting their way, they're better off joining her team than continuing to fight her.

Learning the Difference between Responding and Reacting

As both you and your grandchildren adjust to your new living arrangement, emotions on both sides will run very high. Such stockpiles of built-up feelings can lead us to act on impulse, causing us to make decisions on the spur of the moment or even driving us to blurt out things in the heat of emotion that we may later regret. In any difficult and emotionally charged situation, it's easier for us to keep our wits about us if we understand that there is a difference between responses and reactions.

First, when we react to a person or a situation, we're acting on instinct or reflex, as the term *gut reaction* suggests. For example, when we cover our eyes during the violent climax of a horror film or cringe when we see someone drop a plate, just knowing the sound of the smash is coming, we're reacting to our surroundings without even thinking. These reactions are our body's way of preparing us for, or protecting us from something unpleasant or unwelcome.

Likewise, when someone strikes out at us accusingly, our automatic protection system sends out a signal for us to either fend off or block out the unwelcome experience. As we've established in a previous chapter, any unwelcome assault on our senses, whether auditory or visual, imagined or real, will cause a natural defensive or protective reaction.

In dealing with a child who is acting out or lashing out angrily (unless in a violent manner, of course), the stress this produces in you will be greatly reduced if you learn to pause for a moment, reflect on the situation, and then form a calm and rational response in return. Living under prolonged stress is the emotional equivalent of living under constant attack.

In such circumstances, we never let down our guard. Our emotional defense system stays active at all times, causing us to be forever ready and alert for the next assault. For those who deal daily with the unknown and who must stay prepared at all times for the unexpected, this feeling of being on guard becomes a way of life. The tension of staying prepared for the worst over time leads to what we call *stress*, and *stress* is just the fanciful term we use to describe the physical and emotional toll that living in a perpetual state of defensiveness will take on us. Our sensitivity to the unexpected sharpens our alertness, and we jump at the slightest sound. Living in this state for long periods is physically and mentally draining. Even the best guard can't stay on the lookout for too long without a break and a quick cup of coffee.

When grandparents take in their grandchildren, they're constantly on the lookout because the unknown and the unexpected are all they know. Having an understanding of how your defense system works can help you to gain more control over your stress level, even when you're not able to gain control over your circumstances. A great deal of the stress you feel can be relieved just by becoming aware of your increased sensitivity and learning to use this heightened awareness to your advantage. *Reacting* relieves stress; *responding* prevents it.

With the basic understanding that reactions differ from responses, you have just gained one more tool for dealing more effectively with difficult situations. We can now call on the same skill we used in addressing children's difficult questions to handle their rebellion, testing, acting out behaviors, and emotional outbursts.

As with their questions, when children are acting out in a way that is making you angry or defensive, you should use these feelings as a warning light, cautioning you that it's time to slow down and stop before you respond. To avoid reacting according to what your feelings are telling you, just pause momentarily and reflect on what's going on both inside and outside yourself. Acknowledge that you're feeling angry, hurt, criticized, unappreciated, disrespected, etc., but don't use these feelings to form your response. This momentary pause makes the difference between reacting and responding by putting vital distance between you and your gut-level instinct. Time lets you put reason in the driver's seat. Without the distance this slight pause gives you, the only tool you'd have at your disposal would be the instinctual and defensive voice of your emotions. As a rational adult with a difficult child on your hands, you can't afford to let your feelings do the driving.

Responding requires that you ask yourself what your grandchildren's acting out is really trying to tell you. It's never what it appears to be, and taking it at face value is cheating you both. As with outbursts along the lines of, *"I hate you!"* rebellious and defiant behaviors are messages in disguise. When you use the same principles we discussed in Chapter 5 to address acting out behaviors, it is often enough to lessen the heat of the attack and turn it into a discussion.

Example #1:

A child refuses to clean up his room at his grandmother's repeated requests. He remarks: *"You can't tell me what to do— you're not my mother!"*

The grandmother feels: hurt, betrayed, angry, unappreciated, and disrespected. A defensive reaction would be: *"I can tell you whatever I want to. You're in my home now!"*

When grandparents fail to put some distance between their feelings and their responses, the responses are not responses at all. Remember, responses are dictated by thought; reactions are dictated by feelings.

In the preceding example, the grandmother, too overcome by the feeling of being unappreciated, loses touch with her rational senses. Fearing that a calm approach will give the child the impression that he can walk all over the grandmother and she'll just lie there and take it, the grandmother commands the child to show her a well-deserved and missing sense of respect. But ironically, the child continues to resist her authority, feeling disrespected in kind by the grandmother's counterattack. And the battle rages on.

Lashing back at a child by demanding respect will typically yield the opposite result. Let's consider an alternative way of handling the same situation, tuning more in with what the child is feeling than the grandmother:

Child: *"You can't tell me what to do—you're not my mother!"* The child is feeling: unwanted, helpless, abandoned, and rejected. The child is saying through this behavior: *"I'm angry because someone other than my mother and father is taking care of me and telling me what to do."*

A reflective response would be: *"You must be really mad that someone else has to do your mother and father's job."*

Angry reactions never address the real issues. They serve only to fan the flames and intensify bad feelings. They stem from the grandparents' *feelings* instead of the grandparents' *reasoning* and ability to put themselves in the shoes of their grandchildren. Reflective responses do just that—they *reflect* back to the children what is really going on instead of putting them in their place. They take the wind out of the rebellion by skipping over the surface issue (the behavior) and getting straight to the point.

Example # 2:

Child: *"You're so mean. I want to go back and live with my Mom. At least she let me have some fun!"*

What the grandparent feels: offended, insulted, put down, and unappreciated. Emotional reaction: *"If it weren't for me, you'd be out on the streets. You're just like your mother—neither one of you appreciates anything."*

Here's the same encounter using the new approach:

Child: *"You're so mean. I want to go back and live with my Mom. At least she let me have some fun!"* What the child is feeling: punished, misunderstood, controlled, and restricted. What the child is really saying: *"I'm not used to anyone putting restrictions on me."*

Reflective response: *"You're having trouble understanding that someone who loves you doesn't just let you do whatever you want. It'll be hard for you to get used to the idea that loving someone means sometimes saying 'no' and not just saying 'yes' to try to make them happy."*

These reflective responses may feel awkward, unnatural, or even mechanical at first. But in the long run, they will help you to feel much less stressed and more in control of these skirmishes because they remind you that you don't have to fight every battle. Responding lets you cut through the bluster and get to the heart of the matter with less mess and little stress. Because you refuse to take the bait, and because you stay calm and rational, your grandchildren may use this against you to make you feel like you don't really care. They may poke fun at you, saying things like, *"You sound like a robot—all those books you're reading are taking control of your mind."* But if you know in your heart that you don't have to fight to prove your love, nothing they could say could make you trade back your old ways for the new. Knowing they can get a reaction out of you by pushing the right button gives your grandchildren an incentive to do it often and without mercy. It becomes a game of, *"You hurt me, I hurt you back"*—and this is a game no grandparent should play.

Children who have been neglected will need to test others unremittingly to see if they really do care. Don't let them bait you into rejecting them like they expect you to. There is nothing that reassures children more that you won't be like all the rest and abandon them, than a stubborn refusal to fight back. Your cool and consistently caring approach will tell your grandchildren that, no matter how miserably they behave, you will not play the hurting game.

Distinguishing between Punishment and Consequences

Understand that, in many respects, grandchildren already feel punished before they arrive on your doorstep. Being robbed of a healthy parent-child relationship seems in itself a kind of punishment. When this is the case, and when children feel unwanted by the very people responsible for giving them life, they feel little stability or control in their own lives and may question their very reason for being. Children who have had no say in being born into an already uneasy situation are now left with no say about what becomes of them. Life seems to have dealt them a double blow, having brought them into this world, only to cast them from pillar to post and right into the hands of uncertainty.

When children feel they have no control over their lives and fear that those responsible for making decisions on their behalf are untrustworthy, they learn to become self-reliant and self-sufficient at a very young age. Their only means of gaining some control in the face of such instability is often through their ability to resist the control of others. Many children who have lived for a number of years with disinterested or frequently absent parents have been forced into premature adulthood, taking responsibility for themselves and becoming caretakers to their defective parents. When such children are transplanted into a new environment in which they are suddenly asked to entrust their care to someone else, they are essentially being asked to be children, when they have been acting like adults nearly from the start. Such circumstances give rise to children who have trouble conforming to structure and who are stubbornly independent. To the untrained eye, this deeply-rooted sense of self-reliance is easily mistaken for rebelliousness.

While stubbornness and self-will are not inherently bad traits, they take on different connotations, depending on how they're viewed and how they're put to use. When they're viewed as persistence or perseverance, they are often the only things that drive a person to trudge on through insurmountable hardships. But when viewed as rebelliousness or disobedience, they appear more self-defeating in nature.

Stubbornness and a strong sense of self-will can prove to be an individual's greatest strength or most damaging liability. Life experience teaches us how to channel our stubbornness into a powerful motivational tool, inspiring us to achieve any goal we set or enabling us to overcome any obstacle that blocks our path. When dealing with children and adolescents in particular, we have to stay open to the possibility that they haven't yet learned that fine distinction between rebellion and independence.

This is yet another delicate balancing act for grandparents—finding a way to encourage their grandchildren to be independent without allowing them to be disobedient. From your grandchildren's point of view, there is no difference between conformity and helplessness. To them, they're both the same. If they've learned not to trust anyone other than themselves, just as they've learned that nothing will get done unless they do it themselves, the consequences of them putting their welfare in the hands of the wrong person could prove disastrous. When viewed in this light, their inability to readily accept your concern or adapt to the structure you provide begins to look more like a healthy sense of self-preservation than out and out rebellion.

When we begin to understand why these grandchildren are so reluctant to let go of their old defenses, and why they may have so much difficulty accepting the direction and help of others, we gain a new appreciation of their resistance. You can put this knowledge to use in preserving your grandchildren's sense of control by modifying the way you introduce them to your rules. They'll accept your structure more readily if you've mastered the distinction between punishment and consequences.

Simply put, *punishment* is decided by others, while *consequences* are determined by us alone. In other words, punishment is a penalty handed down by an authority figure, while consequences are the result of our own actions. With punishment, someone else is always in control of delivering the penalty; with consequences, we alone decide the outcome. Punishment alone has never discouraged anyone from breaking rules. Our prisons are filled with individuals who can attest to this.

It's far easier for us to justify breaking a rule if we disagree with it and if the potential payoff in breaking it is greater than the risk of the punishment that looms overhead. If a man feels the amount of tax he must pay is unreasonable, his short-term gain from fudging the figures is well worth the risk, and his reward is much more immediate than the distant prospect of being caught. It's a perfect crime—the rules have been arbitrarily set by an abstract authority so the man feels justified in finding a way around them. Because the rules and the punishment are impersonal, the man feels no shame in cheating the system.

The best way for an authority figure to get others to comply is to personalize the rules and the consequences. This doesn't mean that the government should suddenly allow us to set our own tax rates, but it does mean that as authority figures, grandparents' greatest power lies in empowering their grandchildren. Personalizing the limits they place on them puts the children in control of the outcome. Most of us are much more likely to comply with a rule or a standard if we see that doing so has some concrete benefit to us. We are also more likely to follow standards, particularly those we don't like, if the penalty for defying them is the loss of something of value to us personally. Because the only penalty for speeding is being fined, few people drive within the speed limit. The punishment simply isn't enough to overshadow the benefit of getting to a destination more quickly. If the consequence of speeding, on the other hand, were the immediate suspension of a driver's license, you'd see more people slowing down and planning ahead because something important to the individual would be at stake.

For the most part, the reason children don't see the difference between consequences and punishment is that adults don't see the difference themselves. Even though the penalties in either case may be the same, the subtle difference lies in the way these penalties are presented. When you establish a positive incentive for following a rule, rather than just imposing a consequence for not doing so, you encourage children to make the right choice because of the inherent reward, not because of the impending punishment. Doing the right thing becomes rewarding, while doing the wrong thing means they'll be deprived of something they value. Their choice then, not your power or authority, determines what happens as a result. The way in which you present a situation can make all the difference. Consider the following examples involving a grandmother and her grandson.

Example #1:
Grandmother: *"If you don't pick up your things, you'll have to go without dinner."*
Example #2:
Grandmother: *"When you've picked up your things, we'll be able to have dinner."*

While the expectation and the consequence remain the same in both cases, each statement delivers a very different message. *Example #1* tells the child that the grandmother is in control of determining whether or not he'll eat. *Example #2* tells the child that his own choices will determine whether or not he will join the family for dinner. In the second example, if the child doesn't do as the grandmother says, he'll have only himself to blame if he goes hungry—he was given a clear choice.

When given this kind of choice, the child has to think seriously about whether his need to flex his muscles with his grandmother is more important to him at the moment than eating dinner. Something meaningful to him is at stake here, and if he chooses wisely he loses nothing. *Example #1* on the other hand sets up the possibility that the child will disobey, be deprived of dinner, go hungry, and accuse his grandmother of being mean. In *Example #2*, should the child disobey and go without dinner, the grandmother has an ideal opportunity to remind him, *"I told you what you needed to do and you chose not to do it."* In *Example #2,* the outcome and the consequences remain in the child's hands at all times.

Now consider another illustration.

Example #1:
Grandmother: *"If you don't help me with the dishes, I won't let you go skateboarding with Johnny."*
Example #2:
Grandmother: *"When you've put the dishes away, you can go over to Johnny's to skateboard."*

The power struggle between you and your grandchildren is vastly diminished when you set up your expectations so that their behavior, rather than your authority alone, dictates the outcome. Therefore, the reward or consequence in effect is earned. By doing this, you also help your grandchildren learn early the merit of being responsible individuals who carefully consider their options and make their choices accordingly. Otherwise, they learn to become passive participants in their own lives, forever blaming others when things don't go their way. A crippling attitude of helplessness or a "victim mentality" can develop when children learn that others who are more powerful than they are hold the keys to their fate—that they are weak and powerless and nothing they do will make a difference.

Most importantly, remember that when your grandchildren act out, it is most often a plea for attention or for help. Avoid labeling this behavior as "bad" and therefore deserving of punishment; accept it as "lost" and therefore deserving of direction. Bearing the label of being "bad" has branded many troubled children and robbed them of the opportunity to improve because their cries for direction went unheard.

Punishing children for disobeying without guiding them or teaching them a more appropriate alternative only serves to reinforce their fear, that it is them against the world. Of course, you'll need to be firm and authoritative when necessary, but don't forget that power used without compassion is cruelty.

9

The Grandchild's Perspective

As both the author of this book and one who has withstood the rigors and discovered the unique payoffs of having been brought up in the care of my own grandparents, this is my opportunity to speak to you directly. As only one of the millions of children who are raised in nontraditional home environments, I certainly cannot claim to know what the future has in store for all of you, but perhaps what I can provide for you is the unique opportunity to hear things from a grandchild's point of view.

It would certainly be ideal if my experiences alone gave me the power to predict for you what the end result will be in your family, but this isn't likely. Nonetheless, my hope is that you will be able to benefit from some of my insights and avoid some of the common stumbling blocks I've come across in both my own family experience and in my professional work with similar families.

This book, and this chapter in particular, provide an opportunity for me to give back just a fraction of what I've learned in the spirit that it might give others the help that wasn't available to me or to my grandparents when we needed it the most. Although this book is intended primarily for the benefit of the grandparents who shoulder the majority of responsibility in these cases, this chapter is for the entire family.

Being part of a family, whether traditional or not, is no easy feat for anyone. I hope that each of you can appreciate that as a part of a larger unit, you play double duty as both an individual piece and an interwoven part of the family fabric as a whole. Playing both roles forces each of us to weigh the good of the individual against the good of the whole at all times.

When any member of our family unit is in trouble, the unit is impacted as a whole in some way. We are all affected by what the others in our family do, and vice versa. If correctly done, being part of a family prepares us for our larger role in society by training us to take into consideration the impact our actions will have on the others around us.

All families are different, of course, but what we all have in common is that we are all a gathering of separate and unique characters who have been assigned to play on a common team. When we consider that (except through marriage) we don't get to choose our teammates, and that in spite of our unique personalities and widely varying natures we are expected to function as one cooperative body, it's a wonder we're able to get along at all! What families are asked to do defies all reasoning. When it comes right down to it, families are expected to accomplish what a comparable group of strangers more than likely could not!

Despite their respective quirks, peculiarities, and idiosyncrasies, our families are just that—our families. Certainly, we didn't choose them, but by the same token, we can't trade them in. And if we could, who of sound mind would dream of swapping places with them? If your family is anything like mine, you couldn't pay an outsider enough to put up with what we put each other through at no charge. *Because* we don't choose them, and *because* they're a part of us for life, families force us to take inventory of our strengths and weaknesses, our depth or our shallowness, and our tolerance or intolerance of the imperfections of our fellow human beings. And above all, they teach us the true meaning of obligation, because being part of a family means we inherit a fundamental responsibility to a predetermined set of people with whom we seem at times to have no more in common than our genes. Without our families, we would not be compelled to face these basic truths about ourselves. With families, we face them because we *have* to. Through all their imperfections, thank God for our families!

If in reading the pages of this book you feel I've been unfairly harsh or judgmental, particularly with regard to parents, this has not been my intent. Should you conclude that I've been overly protective of the children at the expense of compassion toward the parents, you've missed my point. I've chosen to capture the real problems of the real families I've worked with professionally and the real families I know personally in their true light. I've chosen an honest, straightforward, and no-nonsense approach because this is simply the reality. Portraying these problems in a softer light simply would not be accurate. If my directness has moved just one person to take a more serious look at the importance of the role she or he plays in the family, I consider this time well spent.

As I have stated in previous chapters, I am abundantly aware that parents are simply people who have children; many of them are people who have children under less than ideal circumstances. Whatever strengths, limitations, faults, or frailties they may have had to begin with, the pressures of parenthood can either bring out the best in people or make their limitations all the more apparent. It is true that as individuals we all bring our share of baggage into any relationship. A parent's relationship with a child is no exception. My advice to everyone is to accept this as fact and move on. If we don't, we will conspire to make our parents' baggage become the burden of generations to come.

My message to those parents who may have children in a grandparent's care is to stay focused on the fact that no matter what your differences may be, as a family you are all on the same team. No matter the circumstances that led you to your present situation, you can't afford to be divided. Stay united in the understanding that together you are working toward a common goal. Remember, you have equal responsibility to the family as a whole and yourself as an individual.

I do understand that it must be both difficult and painful to have a child over whose care you have little say, but you should never allow this pain to drive you into petty power struggles over who has the final say. Not all battles are worth fighting, and with a child on the line, you must choose your battles wisely.

You must rest assured that no one will ever replace you as a parent. No one should try. But also believe that your standing as a parent means nothing more than biology unless you work at it. Never take your relationship with your children for granted. Having the trust, respect, or even the love of your children is never a given—it's just a possibility. Your status as parent doesn't guarantee you any of these things if you haven't earned them. Parents who have put their own pursuits above the needs of their children, only to look bewildered when their children don't believe in them, should not be so surprised. I have found that the single most damning error parents in these situations make is their insistence that their children owe them something. Children and parents alike, will get back as much or as little as they invest in each other. Please remember above all that children don't need their parents to be perfect, they just need their parents to be there.

For those children who are in a grandparent's care, I was once there, too. I know it's not ideal, and it's certainly not what childhood dreams are made of, but I've also found that if you look more closely at what you have and stop worrying about what you haven't got, it makes the whole situation a lot more livable.

My greatest hope for you children is that you learn early on one lesson that took me a lot of heartache to learn—namely, to stop being angry with our family members for not being the people we want them to be and accept them for who they are. People are not put on this planet to be who we want them to be—they're here to be exactly who they are. The sooner we all realize this, the happier we'll be.

I've had to learn the hard way that holding resentments against people because they don't live up to our expectations is the greatest offense we can commit against another person. When we fall into this kind of judgment, our egos are seriously in need of realignment because this thinking implies that other people are put here for our own personal benefit. We should all be that important!

As sensitive beings by nature, many of us seem to have un-limited compassion for our fellow humans, so it's truly a tragedy when we can't apply this compassion to our families. For you children, I sincerely hope that you won't be so short-sighted. I encourage you, if you haven't already done so, to start looking past whatever hurt, whatever anger, and whatever disappointment you might feel and find in your heart the same compassion for your parents you'd so freely offer to a stranger. The world didn't just start spinning the moment you were born, and you have to understand that your parents' lives are much more complex than you may ever know. Unless you have taken the time to really get to know them and to appreciate them in the full context of their experiences, don't be so hasty to judge them on the basis of your limited experience alone.

Unless you believe your parents to be evil or mean-spirited, you have to accept that they have done the best they were *capable* of doing, given their own fears, their own hardships, their own abilities, and the support and information (or lack of it) that was available to them at the time. Few people hurt others intentionally or with malice of forethought. Most of the hurt we experience at the hands of others is not spiteful—it's simply what happens when they don't stop to think about the effect their actions will have on us.

Chances are, your parents didn't set out to heap hurt on you, but you've most likely been hurt nonetheless. Do yourself a favor and learn an important lesson from them—one that they might not have known themselves: that perhaps the biggest mistake we all make in our lives is thinking more about what we want in the moment and not enough about how this may come back to haunt us or others down the road.

None of this is said to make light of the pain you may feel at bearing the brunt of such mistakes, nor is it said to diminish the anger or disappointment you might feel. It's said to help you understand that your best hope of someday freeing yourself from the prison of these feelings is to stop blaming your parents for their lack of foresight.

Accept them in spite of their imperfections because, in adulthood, you'll certainly expect them to do the same for you. In order for children to stay angry at their parents for a lifetime, they have to believe somehow that their parents had clear choices and purposefully chose the path that caused them hurt and disappointment. Holding onto this long-term anger requires that they truly believe the path of pain was chosen in the face of clear alternatives.

If you look around you and find yourself saying things like, *"Things could have been different,"* or your parents just *"should have known better,"* you do both your parents and yourself a grave disservice. It is my experience that each of us can only make the choices we're capable of making at any given time. We can't judge the choices we've made (or those anyone else has made, for that matter) by our present knowledge because we didn't know then what we know now. It's typically the mistakes we make that give us the knowledge and understanding we now have.

The wisdom of experience isn't available to us until we've earned it. This shouldn't stop us from putting the experience we've earned to good use once we've got it, but we need to stop judging ourselves and others by what we feel they *should* have known. Simply put, if your parents *could* have done things differently, they probably would have.

If my experience has shown me that parents are most guilty of demanding their children's respect when there is no evidence of why they should have it, then what I've found these children are most guilty of is having unrealistic and superhuman expectations of their parents. Many of us hang onto the hypocritical belief that it's okay for others to make mistakes or bad choices, but our parents should somehow know better. This just isn't logical.

What it does clearly tell us, though, is how very hard it is for us to give up our childhood fantasy that it's our parents' duty to create a perfect, trouble-free world for us. Many of us find out all too soon that our fantasies are just fantasies when they're shattered by the reality of human limitations. But it's unfair for children of any age to hold their parents to a standard of perfection that no one is capable of reaching.

As you grow older, I hope you'll come to appreciate that your parents and your grandparents may give you less than you'd hoped for but far more than you realize.

Parents have their own personal responsibility to make good on the mistakes they've made, but children have a similar responsibility not to allow those mistakes to hold them back in their own lives. As children, we weren't able to choose where or when we came into the world or in what circumstances we'd end up. We didn't get our pick of parents or have the privilege of hand-selecting our family members. But that doesn't mean we're less responsible for becoming the best person we can be. If we can't succeed *because* of our circumstances, we have to succeed *in spite* of them.

Rather than cursing our hardships, we should embrace them, for these are the challenges that will either cripple us or inspire us. That our parents are imperfect is irrelevant when it comes to determining what path our individual lives will take. My particular experience with surviving less than ideal circumstances has brought me to two very important conclusions that I hope will be of some help to each of you as well.

First:

- *Not having a choice in any given matter does not excuse us from dealing with it in a dignified and straightforward manner.*

Like it or not, not having a choice in our lot in life is simply the way it is. As humans, none of us has complete control over the events that shape our lives. Those who try to gain this kind of control suffer more than their fair share of disappointments. In many respects, that we can't control these events is good because we are not always the best judges of what is in our own best interest.

Don't make the same mistake I've seen so many others make, in that they feel it's somehow unfair for them to be expected to deal with anything they didn't want to happen. In actual fact, it's not the ordinary, day-to-day routine experiences of living that make us strong. True character and commitment are only revealed when we're put to the test. Only truly extraordinary events can create truly extraordinary people. When we think about the people we admire most, we don't think of those who've managed to muddle through the mundane drudgery of everyday existence, but rather, it's those who have faced great obstacles and faced them with courage.

No matter your place in the family, and no matter the part you played or did not play in creating the challenging circumstances that surround you, you have been given the gift of free will. It is your choice and yours alone that will determine how you will face the obstacles in your life. You can either choose to stay angry or bitter because your own poor choices or those of others have landed you in a muddle, or you can meet your adversity head-on with the rugged determination that it won't be enough to lay to ruins your spirit or you future. Blaming others for the problems we're faced with may give us some satisfaction, in that we can forever remind those responsible of what they've done to us, but it is certainly no way to live.

The second and final conclusion I've reached is this:

• _Responsibility_ and _accountability_ are two different things.

Understanding that responsibility and accountability are two very different concepts allows us all to rest a bit easier when it comes to the future of those we love. This means specifically that, as children, we are not _responsible_ for what happens to us or around us. We are no more responsible for the problems that began before we came along than we are for fixing them. We are not _responsible_ for the abuse or neglect we may have suffered at the hands of others, because nothing a child could possibly do could warrant these kinds of acts. In childhood, we are not _responsible_ for the thoughtless deeds of others, for as children we are at their mercy and are, for the only time in our lives, truly helpless.

But no matter what evils may have befallen us, we are nonetheless _accountable_ for what we make of them in the long run. If we are survivors of abuse, abandonment, neglect, or other misfortunes, we certainly cannot take _responsibility_ for these, but we must at some point become _accountable_ for ourselves as individuals in spite of them. Even though these scars have been indelibly etched on us by others, they can't ever be erased. They remain forever a part of who we are.

We are all products of our unique experiences, and our experiences shape and mold the people we eventually become. But it is truly unfortunate when people somehow fail to realize that these experiences, though a part of who they are, do not make up the sum total of their being.

For grandparents, parents, and grandchildren alike, I hope you'll come to understand and believe in genuine _accountability_.

If you do, perhaps you won't be so hasty the next time you find yourself excusing someone's behavior on the grounds that he or she suffered too much abuse in the past. Being a victim of tragedy is unfortunate, but it doesn't give us the right to be irrational, irresponsible, or insensitive in the here and now. And it certainly doesn't give us the right to continue willfully playing the victim in our lives today.

Grandparent—no matter what hardships you fear lie ahead for you and your grandchildren, you must be comforted that it is your grandchildren and them alone who will be the judge of how these events will affect them in their later years. And if it is your adult children who wave the banner of irresponsibility because of the ills you exposed them to as children, you must understand that no matter what you may or may not have done, it is their conscious choice to continue playing the victim today. Blaming you is just a convenient way to avoid growing up and becoming accountable for themselves. They have the power to forgive you for not having known better, just as their children may someday forgive them.

One thing we can certainly all learn from the grandparents who raise us is the spirit of true commitment. By nobly putting their own plans on hold, they show us how to put aside what we *want* to do, in order to do what we *must*. They also show us that what we *have* is far less important than what we can *give*. And perhaps most importantly, they teach us that what we *want* is secondary to what is *right*.

Being raised under unconventional circumstances means that things don't come easy for us, but no one knows better than we do that when our victories are hard fought and hard won, they will never be taken for granted.

Appendix A

General Resources

Please note: the website addresses provided here are current as of the date of publication; however, the reader is advised to be aware of the fact that such addresses change frequently.

AARP Grandparent Information Center
601 E St. NW
Washington, DC 20049
Tel: (202) 434-2296 weekdays 9:00 to 5:00 EST
Fax: (202) 434-6474
Website: http://www.aarp.org
National organization providing information and referral to grandparents raising grandchildren. Publishes newsletter, pamphlets, brochures, fact sheets, and other informative materials. Referrals to support groups.

African American Family Services
2616 Nicollett Ave. South
Minneapolis, MN 55408
Tel: (612) 871-7878; Fax: (612) 871-2567

Big Brothers/Big Sisters of America
230 N. 13th St.
Philadelphia, PA 19107
Tel: (215) 567-7000; Fax: (215) 567-0394
Website: http://www.bbbsa.org
Write or call for information or consult your local telephone directory.

Center for Children of Incarcerated Parents
714 W. California Blvd.
Pasadena, CA 91105
Tel: (626) 397-1396

Child Welfare League of America
440 First St. NW, Third Floor
Washington, DC 20001-2085
Tel: (202) 638-2952; Fax: (202) 638-4004
Website: http://www.cwla.org
Membership association of public and private organizations providing services to at risk children and youths.

DHHS Administration on Aging
US Dept. of Health and Human Services
330 Independence Ave. SW
Washington, DC 20201
Tel: (202) 619-0724; Fax: (202) 260-1012
National Aging Information Center Line: (202) 619-7501
Website: http://www.aoa.dhhs.gov

Families Anonymous
P.O. Box 528
Van Nuys, CA 91408
Tel: (818) 989-7841
Self-help group for families and friends of people with behavioral problems. Write or call for information or consult your local telephone directory.

Foundation for Grandparenting
5 Cassa del Oro Lane
Santa Fe, NM 87505
Tel: (505) 466-1336; Fax: same
Contact: Arthur Kornhaber, MD
E-mail: gpfound@trail.com
Website: http://www.grandparenting.org
Information, networking, and research regarding all aspects of grandparent-grandchild-parent relationships. Newsletter *Vital Connections,* grandparent-grandchild summer camp. For information, send SASE with two 1st class stamps to:
Foundation for Grandparenting
7 Avenida Vista Grande, Suite B7-160
Santa Fe, NM 87505.

Generations United
440 First St. NW, Suite 310
Washington, DC 20001-2085
Tel: (202) 662-4283; Fax: (202) 408-7629
Website: http://www.gu.org
An international coalition dedicated to intergenerational policy, programs, and issues.

Grandparent Rights Organization
555 S. Old Woodward Ave., Suite 600
Birmingham, MI 48009
Tel: (248) 646-7191; Fax: (248) 646-9722
Clearinghouse for state laws affecting grandparents raising their grandchildren and issues pertaining to grandparent visitation rights. National newsletter. Legal services available through: Richard S. Victor, Attorney at Law, at the above address. Telephone (248) 646-7177.

Head Start Bureau
Switzer Bldg., Room 2050
330 C St. SW
Washington, DC 20201
Tel: (202) 205-8572
Website: http://www.acf.dhhs.gov/programs/hsb/index.htm
Head Start programs provide social, medical, dental, mental health, and other services to low-income children and their families. Write for directory of programs or consult your local telephone directory. Website offers information on programs and services, current initiatives, events, and resource library.

Legal Services for Prisoners with Children
100 McAllister St.
San Francisco, CA 94102
Tel: (415) 255-7036; Fax: (415) 552-3150

National Coalition of Grandparents, Inc.
137 Larkin St.
Madison, WI 53705
Tel: (608) 238-8751; Fax: same
Contact: Ethel Dunn. E-mail: sedun@inxpress.net
Website:http://www.geocities.com/heartland/prairie/6866/index.html
Consortium of individuals seeking to effect legislative change. Assists those grandparents and other kin raising children, and grandparents/grandchildren who have been denied access to each other.

National Council on Aging, Inc.
409 Third St., SW, Suite 200
Washington, DC 20024
Tel: (202) 479-1200
Website: http://www.ncoa.org
Private, non-profit organization promoting the well-being of the aging population.

National Council on Family Relations
3989 Central Ave., NE, Suite 550
Minneapolis, MN 55421
Tel: (888) 781-9331, (612) 781-9331; Fax: (612) 781-9348
A forum for family researchers, educators, and practitioners to share information about families and family relationships.

National Family Caregivers Association
10605 Concord St., Suite 501
Kensington, MD 20805-2504
Tel: (800) 896-3650; Fax: (301) 942-2302
Membership organization offering information, education, support, public awareness, and advocacy to families caring for relatives with chronic illness or disability.

National Self-Help Clearinghouse
25 W. 43rd St., Room 620
New York, NY 10036
Tel: (212) 642-2944
Information and referral service providing information about self-help groups, helping networks, and community support services.

Non-Custodial Parent and Grandparent Organization
P.O. Box 1169
Grand Rapids, MI 49501-1169

Parents Anonymous National Headquarters
675 W. Foothill Blvd., Suite 220
Claremont, CA 91711
Tel: (909) 621-6184; Fax: (909) 625-6304
Info line: (800) 339-6993
Modified self-help group for parents. Not a twelve-step group.
Write or call for information.

Parents Helping Parents, (PHP) Family Resource Center, Inc.
3041 Olcott St.
Santa Clara, CA 95054-3222
Tel: (408) 727-5775; Fax: (408) 727-0182
Website: http://www.php.com
National resource center offering information, newsletters, special
needs library, resource database, parenting groups, including grandparent support group. Comprehensive, multilingual services for
children with special needs and their families.

Tough Love
P.O. Box 1069
Doylestown, PA 18901
Tel: (800) 333-1069; (215) 348-7090
Website: http://www.toughlove.org
Self-help groups for families of troubled children.

Appendix B

Help with Specific Problems

Alcohol and Drug Dependency and Addiction

Al-Anon and Al-Ateen Family Group National Headquarters
1600 Corporate Landing Parkway
Virginia Beach, VA 23454-5617
Tel: (800) 356-9996
Website: http://www.al-anon-alateen.org
Self-help groups for family members of alcoholics. Multilingual helpline. Write or call for listings or consult your local telephone directory. Website has information and links for groups worldwide.

Alcoholics Anonymous General Services Office
P.O. Box 459, Grand Central Station
New York, NY 10063
Tel: (212) 870-3400
Website: http://www.alcoholics-anonymous.org
Worldwide fellowship of recovering alcoholics. Write or call for information or consult your local telephone directory.

American Council on Alcoholism, Inc.
2522 St. Paul Street
Baltimore, MD 21218
Tel: (800) 527-5344

American Council for Drug Education
164 W. 74th St.
New York, NY 10023
Tel: (800) 488-3784, (212) 595-5810 ext. 7860
Website: http://www.drughelp.org
Bilingual. Educational materials and publications.

Children of Alcoholics Foundation
P.O. Box 4185, Grand Central Station
New York, NY 10163-4185
Tel: (800) 359-2623, (212) 754-0656
Information designed to increase public awareness of the effects of alcoholism on the family. Hotline provides referrals to national and local self-help groups, counseling services, and treatment centers.

CoAnon Family Groups
Self-help groups for families of cocaine abusers. Consult your local telephone directory for local listings.

Cocaine Anonymous
3740 Overland Ave., Suite G
Los Angeles, CA 90034
Tel: (800) 347-8998
Website: http://www.ca.org
Self-help groups for cocaine abusers. National referral line. Write or call for listings or consult your local telephone directory.

Gamblers Anonymous World Service Office
P.O. Box 17173
Los Angeles, CA 90017
Tel: (323) 386-8789
Self-help groups for problem gamblers. National referral line. Write or call for listings or consult your local telephone directory.

Gamanon National Headquarters
Tel: (718) 352-1671
Self-help group for family members of problem gamblers. Call for listings or consult your local telephone directory.

Marijuana Anonymous
P.O. Box 2912
Van Nuys, CA 91404
Tel: (800) 766-6779
Website: http://www.marijuana-anonymous.org
Self-help groups for marijuana abusers. Write or call for listings or consult your local telephone directory.

Mothers Against Drunk Driving (MADD)
511 E. John Carpenter Freeway, Suite 700
Irvine, TX 75062
Tel: (800) GET-MADD, (214) 744-6233; Fax: (214) 869-2206
Website: http://www.madd.org

NarAnon Family Groups
P.O. Box 2562
Palos Verdes Peninsula, CA 90274
Tel: (310) 547-5800
Self-help groups for family members of narcotics abusers. Write or call for information or consult your local telephone directory.

Narcotics Anonymous World Service Office
19737 Nordhoff Place
Chatsworth, CA 91311
Tel: (818) 773-9999
Website: http://www.na.org
Self-help groups for narcotics abusers. Write or call for listings or consult your local telephone directory.

National Association for Children of Alcoholics
11426 Rockville Pike, Suite 100
Rockville, MD 20852
Tel: (301) 468-0985

National Clearinghouse for Alcohol and Drug Information
11426 Rockville Pike, Suite 200
Rockville, MD 20852
Tel: (800) 729-6686, (301) 468-2600
Bilingual. Write or call for catalog of publications.

National Council on Alcoholism and Drug Dependence
12 W. 21st St.
New York, NY, 10010
Tel: (800) 622-2255
Offers referrals for counseling and treatment, general information, and publications list.

Students Against Driving Drunk
P.O. Box 800
Marlboro, MA 01752
Tel: (508) 481-3568; Fax: (508) 481-5759

Attention Deficit Disorders, Learning Disabilities, and Behavioral Problems

Attention Deficit Information Network, Inc.
475 Hillside Ave.
Needham, MA 02194
Tel: (781) 455-9895; Fax: (781) 444-5466
Website: http://www.addinfonetwork.com
Support groups and information.

Children and Adults with Attention Deficit Disorder (CHADD)
499 NW 70th Ave., Suite 101
Plantation, FL 33317
Tel: (800) 233-4050, (954) 587-3700; Fax: (954) 587-4599
Website: http://www.chadd.org
Membership organization. Offers local, state, and national resources, treatment information, newsletter, publications, and support groups. Free information packet available upon request.

Learning Disabilities Association of America
4156 Library Road
Pittsburgh, PA 15234-1349
Tel: (412) 341-1515
Information and publications on learning disabilities. Has affiliates in all 50 states.

National Attention Deficit Disorder Association
P.O. Box 488
West Newbury, MA 01985
Tel: (800) 487-2282, (440) 350-9595; Fax: (440) 350-0223
Website: http://www.add.org
Information and referrals. Support group listings.

National Center for Learning Disabilities
381 Park Ave. South, Suite 1240
New York, NY 10016
Tel: (212) 545-7510; Fax: (212) 545-9665
Information, advocacy, and publications on learning disabilities.
Offers referrals to local services.

National Information Center for Children and Youth with Disabilities
P.O. Box 1492
Washington, DC 20013
Tel: (800) 695-0285
Call or write for publications list. Offers information on all disabilities and special education related issues.

Child Abuse, Neglect, and Exploitation, Domestic Violence

National Center for Missing and Exploited Children
2101 Wilson Blvd., Suite 550
Arlington, VA 22201-3052
24 hour line for reporting missing children: (800) 843-5678
Tel: (800) 826-7653, (703) 235-3900; Fax: (703) 235-4067
Help locating missing children and preventing child exploitation.

National Coalition Against Domestic Violence
P.O. Box 18749
Denver, CO 80218-0749
Tel: (303) 839-1852; Fax: (303) 831-9251
Website: http://www.ncadv.org
Advocacy for battered women, publications list, and directory of services nationwide.

National Council on Child Abuse and Family Violence
1155 Connecticut Ave. NW, Suite 300
Washington, DC 20036
Tel: (800) 222-2000, (202) 429-6695

HIV/AIDS

Center for Disease Control National AIDS Clearinghouse
P.O. Box 6003
Rockville, MD 20850
Tel: (800) 458-5231
Bilingual. Answers any questions and distributes educational materials on HIV/AIDS. Offers information on organizations providing services for HIV/AIDS. Has automatic Fax-back for quick answers to questions.

Center for Disease Control National AIDS Hotline
P.O. Box 13827
Research Triangle Park, NC 27709
Tel: (800) 342-2437, Spanish Tel: (800) 344-7432
Answers questions and provides information on HIV/AIDS transmission and prevention. Referrals and information packets available.

National Minority AIDS Council
1931 13th St., NW
Washington, DC 20009-4432
Tel: (202) 483-NMAC
Website: http://www.nmac.org
Information on AIDS and its impact on the minority community.

Mental Illness and Homelessness

National Alliance for the Mentally Ill (NAMI)
200 N. Glebe Road, Suite 1015
Arlington, VA 22203-3754
Tel: (800) 950-NAMI
Website: http://www.nami.org
Advocacy, education, and support group information for the mentally ill and their families. Referrals to local chapters.

NAMI Homeless and Missing Service
220 1/2 Putnam St.
Marietta, OH 45750
Tel: (740) 373-3445; Fax: (740) 374-3880
Sponsored by National Alliance for the Mentally Ill, helps families locate homeless or missing persons with mental illness.

National Mental Health Association
1021 Prince St.
Alexandria, VA 22314-2971
Tel: (703) 684-7722; Fax: (703) 684-5968
National Mental Health Association Information Center:
(800) 969-NMHA

National Mental Health Consumer Self-Help Clearinghouse
311 S. Juniper St., Room 902
Philadelphia, PA 19107
Tel: (800) 688-4226, option #3
Self-help, advocacy, information, and referral for families of children with emotional or behavioral problems.

National Resource Center on Homelessness and Mental Illness
262 Delaware Ave.
Delmar, NY 12054
Tel: (800) 444-7415; Fax: (518) 439-7612

Miscellaneous Medical Problems

ALS Association (Lou Gehrig's Disease)
21021 Ventura Blvd., Suite 321
Woodland Hills, CA 91364
Tel: (800) 782-4747
Provides information and referrals to ALS patients and their families.

American Kidney Fund
6110 Executive Blvd., Suite 1010
Rockville, MD 20852
Tel: (800) 638-8299; Fax: (301) 881-0898, (301) 881-3311
Website: http://www.akfinc.org
Information on kidney disease and organ donor programs. Financial assistance available to kidney patients. Educational information available.

American Liver Foundation
1425 Pompton Ave.
Cedar Grove, NJ 07009
Tel: (800) 223-0179
Information and referrals for people with liver disease. Provides referrals to specialists and support groups.

Lupus Foundation of America
4 Research Place, Suite 180
Rockville, MD 20850-3226
Tel: (800) 558-0121, (301) 670-9292
Provides referrals to local chapters. Educational materials and publications available. Call or consult your local telephone directory for local chapter.

National Association of Kidney Patients
100 S. Ashley Dr., Suite 280
Tampa, FL 33602
Tel: (800) 749-2257
Information for kidney patients and their families.

National Multiple Sclerosis Society
30 W. 26th St., 9th Floor
New York, NY 10010
Tel: (800) 344-4867
Website: http://www.nmss.org
Provides general information and referrals to local support groups.

National Sickle Cell Disease Association of America
200 Corporate Drive, Suite 495
Culver City, CA 90230
Tel: (800) 421-8453, (310) 216-6363
Membership organization. Offers information, services, and educational materials.

Runaways and Troubled Youth

National Clearinghouse on Families and Youth
P.O. Box 13505
Silver Spring, MD 20911-3505
Tel: (301) 608-8098
Call for brochure and publications list.

National Organization on Adolescent Pregnancy, Parenting and Prevention
1310 F St. NW, Suite 401
Washington, DC 20004
Tel: (202) 783-5770; Fax: (202) 783-5775

Violent Crime, Gang Violence, Death, and Trauma

Center for Community Change
1000 Wisconsin Ave. NW
Washington, DC 20007
Tel: (202) 342-0519, Fax: (202) 342-1132

Community Youth Gang Service Project, Inc. (Los Angeles County)
144 S. Fetterly Ave.
Los Angeles, CA 90022
Consult your local telephone directory for local projects.

Compassionate Friends
P.O. Box 3696
Oak Brook, IL 60522-3696
Tel: (630) 990-0010
Website: http://www.compassionatefriends.org
Support groups for anyone grieving the loss of a child. Call, check website, or consult your local telephone directory for listings. Also offers resource list of books, pamphlets, and tapes as well as a newsletter for grieving parents and siblings.

Juvenile Justice Clearinghouse
Box 6000
Rockville, MD 20849-6000
Tel: (800) 638-8736; Fax: (301) 519-5212

National Victim Center
2111 Wilson Blvd., Suite 300
Arlington, VA 22201
Tel: (703) 276-2880
Information and referrals to local support services for those who have been victimized.

National Youth Gang Center
Institute for Intergovernmental Research
P.O. Box 12729
Tallahassee, FL 32317
Tel: (850) 385-0600; Fax: (850) 386-5356
Website: http://www.iir.com/nygc

Sidran Foundation
2328 W. Joppa Road, Suite 15
Lutherville, MD 21093
Tel: (410) 825-8888
Website: http://www.sidran.org
Information, advocacy, and publications for adults and children affected by trauma and experiencing trauma-related disorders.

Appendix C

Hotlines

Alcohol and Drug Abuse Helpline
Tel: (800) 821-4357, (800) 821-HELP
Offers referrals to local services and self-help groups.

Alcohol and Drug Abuse Hotline
Tel: (800) 252-6465

ALS Association
Tel: (800) 782-4747
Information about Lou Gehrig's disease.

American Cancer Society
Tel: (800) ACS-2345

American Lupus Society
Tel: (800) 331-1802

Attention Deficit Disorder Hotline
Tel: (800) 254-8081

Boys Town National Hotline
Tel: (800) 448-3000
Bilingual. National hotline for youth problems. Boys Town also operates a number of facilities offering services to children and their families in 13 states.

Cancer Information Service
Tel: (800) 4-CANCER

Childhelp U.S.A.
24-hour National Child Abuse Hotline
Tel: (800) 422-4453, 1-800-4-A-CHILD
Offers crisis counseling, child abuse reporting information, and referrals for every county in the U.S.

Cocaine Hotline
Tel: (800) COCAINE

Families Anonymous
Tel: (800) 736-9805

Grief Recovery Helpline
Tel: (800) 445-4808

Mothers Against Drunk Driving
Tel: (800) GET-MADD

National Adoption Hotline
Tel: (202) 328-1200
Hotline sponsored by The National Committee for Adoption providing referrals to state adoption resources.

National AIDS Hotline
Tel: (800) 342-AIDS, Spanish Tel: (800) 344-7432
Provides basic information on HIV/AIDS, transmission, testing, prevention, referrals, etc.

National Brain Injury Association Family Helpline
Tel: (800) 444-6443
Information and resources for people with head injuries and their families.

National Center for Missing and Exploited Children
Tel: (800) 843-5678
Bilingual.

National Domestic Violence Hotline
Tel: (800) 799-7233

National Runaway Switchboard
Tel: (800) 621-4000
24-hour hotline, crisis intervention for youth and their families.

National Youth Hotline
Tel: (800) 999-9999
24-hour national hotline for runaways and troubled youths and their families. Offers referrals to local services.

National Youth Crisis Hotline
Tel: (800) 422-0009

Parent Hotline
Tel: (800) 356-6767
Referrals to organizations that can assist parents with troubled children.

Substance Abuse Hotline
Tel: (800) 284-1248

Teen Help
Tel: (800) 637-0701
Referral line for parents of adolescents.

ToughLove International
Tel: (800) 333-1069

Appendix D

Suggested Reading

Achieving Grandparent Potential: Viewpoints on Building Intergenerational Relationships, by Robert D. Stron and Shirley K. Strom. Sage, 1992.
ISBN# 0803945124

A Nolo's Pocket Guide to Family Law, by Robin D. Leonard and Stephen Elias. Berkeley, CA: Nolo Press, 1996.
ISBN# 0-87337-322-7

Black Grandparents as Parents, by Lenora Madison Poe. Berkeley, CA: Lenora Madison Poe, 1992.
ISBN# 0-9633992-0-9

The Changing Family, by Mark Hutter. Prentice Hall, 1997.
ISBN# 0023592524

Children of Incarcerated Parents, by Gabel and Johnston. New York: Free Press, 1995.
ISBN# 0-02-911042-4

Connecting the Generations: Grandparenting for the New Millennium, by Dr. Hanks Roma and Stan Dark. The Warren Featherbone Foundation, 1997.
ISBN# 096510719

Contemporary Grandparenting: A Comprehensive Textbook, by Arthur Kornhaber. Newbury Park, CA: Sage, 1995.
ISBN# 0-8039-5805-6, # 0-8039-5806-4

Dangerous Legacy: The Babies of Drug-Taking Parents, by Ben Sonder. Watts, 1994.
ISBN# 0-531-11195-4

Do I Have a Daddy? A Story About a Single Child, by Jeanne Warren Lindsay. Buena Park, CA.: Morning Glory, 1991.
ISBN# 0-930934-45-8

Driven to Distraction: Recognizing and Coping with Attention Deficit Disorder from Childhood Through Adulthood, by Edward M. Hollowell and John Ratey. Simon and Schuhster, 1995.
ISBN# 0684801280

Everything You Need to Know About Living With a Grandparent, by Carolyn Simpson. Rosen Pub., 1995.
ISBN# 0823918726

Grandmothers as Caregivers: Raising the Children of the Crack Cocaine Epidemic, by Meredith Minkler and Kathleen M. Roe. Newbury Park, CA: Sage, 1993.
ISBN# 0-8039-4846-8, # 0-8039-4847-6

Grandparenting, by Sharon Wegscheider-Cruse. Science and Behavior, 1996.
ISBN# 0-8314-0085-4

Grandparenting: A Survival Guide: How Better to Understand Yourself, Your Children and Your Children's Children, by Margery Fridstein. Tageh Press, 1997.
ISBN# 0963838520

Grandparenting by Grace: A Guide Through the Joys and Struggles, by Irene Endicott. Broadman, 1994.
ISBN# 0-8054-6149-3

Grandparenting in a Changing World, by Eda J. LeShan. Newmarket Press, 1996.
ISBN# 1-55704-307-8

Grandparenting Redefined: Guidance for Today's Changing Family, by Irene M. Endicott. Lynwood, WA: Aglow Publications, 1992.
ISBN# 0932305938

Grandparenting with Love and Logic: Practical Solutions to Today's Grandparenting Challenges, by Jim Fay and Foster W. Cline. Golden, CO: Love and Logic Press, 1994.
ISBN# 0-944634-06-0

Grandparent Power: How to Strengthen the Vital Connection Among Grandparents, Parents and Children, by Arthur Kornhaber and Sondra Forsyth. Random House Value, 1995.
ISBN# 0517-88455-0

Grandparents: An Annotated Bibliography on Roles, Rights and Relationships, by Carol Ann Strauss. Scarecrow Press, 1996.
ISBN# 0-8108-3135-x

Grandparents as Parents: A Survival Guide for Raising a Second Family, by Sylvie de Toledo and Deborah Edler Brown. New York: Guilford Press, 1995.
ISBN# 1-57230-011-6, # 1-57230-020-5

Grandparents' Rights, by Jill Manthorpe and Celia Atherton. Age Concern, 1989.
ISBN# 0-86242-079-2

Grandparents' Rights: With Forms (Take the Law Into your Own Hands), by Traci Truly. Clearwater, FL: Sphinx Publications, 1995.
ISBN# 1-57248-001-7

Grandparent Visitation Disputes: A Legal Resource Manual, edited by Ellen C. Segal and Naomi Karp. Washington, D.C.: American Bar Association, 1989.
ISBN# 0-89707-430-0

Gran-Gran's Trick: A Story for Children Who Have Lost Someone They Love, by Dwight Holden and Michael Chesworth. Magination Press, 1989.
ISBN# 0945354193

The Guardianship Book: How to Become a Child's Guardian in California, by David Brown and Lisa Goldoftas. Second edition, Berkeley, CA: Nolo Press, 1997.
ISBN# 0-87337-302-2

Helping Your Grandchildren Through Their Parents' Divorce, by Joan Schrager Cohen. New York, NY: Walker and Company, 1994. ISBN# 0-8027-1298-3, # 0-8027-7433-4

How it Feels When a Parent Dies, by Jill Krementz. Peter Smith, 1993.
ISBN# 0-8446-6675-0

It's Nobody's Fault: New Hope and Help for Difficult Children and Their Parents, by Harold S. Koplewicz, M.D. Times Books, 1996.
ISBN# 0812924738

The Joy of Grandparenting, by Joan Holleman and Audrey Sherins. Meadowbrook Books, 1995.
ISBN# 0-88166-232-1, # 0-88166-232-9, # 0-871-52699-5

The Joy of Grandparenting: Grandparents Make a Difference, by Clarice C. Orr. Bageforde Pub., 1995.
ISBN# 1-886225-00-1

Raising Our Children's Children, by Deborah Doucette-Dudman and Jeffrey LaCure. Minneapolis, MN: Fairview Press, 1996.
ISBN# 0-925190-91-8

Relatives Raising Children: An Overview of Kinship Care, by Joseph D. Crumbley, D.S.W., and Robert L. Little, M.S.W., A.C.S.W. Child Welfare League of America, 1997.
ISBN# 0878686843

The Resilient Self: How Survivors of Troubled Families Rise Above Adversity, by Sybil Wolin, Ph.D. and Steven J. Wolin. Villard Books, 1993.
ISBN# 0394583574

Robert Lives With His Grandparents, by Martha Whitmore Hickman. Albert Whitman and Co. Publishers, 1995.
ISBN# 0-8075-7084-2

The Survival Guide for Kids With LD: Learning Differences, by Gary L. Fisher, Ph.D. and Rhonda Woods Cummings, Ed.D. Free Spirit Pub., 1990.
ISBN# 0-915793-18-0, # 0-915793-20-2

Troubled Transplants: Unconventional Strategies for Helping Disturbed Foster and Adoptive Children, by Richard J. Delaney, Ph.D. and Frank R. Kunstal, Ed.D. Univ. South ME, 1993.
ISBN# 0-939561-14-x, # 0-939561-15-8

Appendix E

Related Publications

A Grandparent's Guide to Family Nurturing and Safety. U.S. Consumer Product Safety Commission (CPSC) in conjunction with the Pamper's Parenting Institute. Tel: (719) 948-4000. Order CPSC item #606E free. On-line version available at:
http://www.cpsc.gov.cpscpub/pubs/grand/grand.htm
Search the website at http://www.cpsc.gov for other articles related to grandparenting.

Formal and Informal Kinship Care Volume I. Narrative Reports and Volume II. Tables and Figures
U.S. Department of Health and Human Services
Office of the Assistant Secretary of Planning and Evaluation
Division of Children and Youth Policy
200 Independence Ave., SW, Room 450G
Washington, DC 20201
Fax requests for report to: (202) 690-5514

Grandparent Caregivers: A National Guide. Available online at:
http://www.igc.org/justice/cjc/spc/manual/cover.html

Grandparenting: Some Facts that You May Not Know
Behavioral and Social Research Program
National Institute on Aging
Gateway Bldg., Suite 533
Bethesda, MD 20892

Grandparents As Parents and *Grandparents' Guide to Navigating the Legal System.* National Committee to Preserve Social Security and Medicare. Tel: (800) 966-1935.

Grandparents Raising Grandchildren Resource Kit
The Child Development Policy Advisory Committee
915 Capitol Mall, Room 336
Sacramento, CA 95814
Tel: (916) 653-3725; Fax: (916) 446-9643

Grandparents Raising Grandchildren: A Guide to Finding Help and Hope, by Marianne Takas
The National Foster Parent Association, Inc.
9 Dartmoor Drive
Crystal Lake, IN 60004
Tel: (815) 455-2527
Send $3.00 plus $1.00 for postage and handling.

Manual for Grandparents and Caregivers, by Ellen Barry, Dorsey Nunn, Carrie Kojimoto, Nancy Jacot-Bell and Gabriela Lujan. Third edition. San Francisco: Legal Services for Prisoners with Children, 1993.

National Directory of Children, Youth and Families Services
P.O. Box 1837
Longmont, CO 80502-1837
Annual directory listing over 30,000 agencies, national organizations, clearinghouses, federal resources, hotlines, and referral information.

Public School Residency Requirements for Students Living on their Own or with Non-Parent, Non-Guardian Caretakers
The Center for Law and Education, Dept. PU
1875 Connecticut Ave. NW, #510
Washington, DC 20009
Fax request to: (202) 462-7687

Public Welfare Directory
American Public Welfare Association
810 First St. NE, Suite 500
Washington, DC 20002-4267
Tel: (202) 682-0100; Fax: (202) 289-6555
Annual directory listing state and local human service agencies including family support, children's and adoption services, and Medicaid resources.

Appendix F

Newsletters

Creative Grandparenting
Creative Grandparenting, Inc.
1003 Delaware Ave., Suite 16
Wilmington, DE 19806
Newsletter and other publications.

Grandparents Journal
1419 E. Marietta Ave.
Spokane, WA 99207-5026

Grandparents Parenting
The Phoenix Foundation
1500 W. El Camino, Suite 325
Sacramento, CA 95833
Tel: (916) 922-1615; Fax: (916) 922-4320

Mature Outlook
1716 Locust St.
Des Moines, IA 50309-3323
Tel: (515) 284-2007

*Off Our Rockers: A Newsletter For Grandparents Raising Their
Children's Children*
P.O. Box 17516
West Palm Beach, FL 33416
Tel: (561) 683-0226; Fax: (561) 615-0996
Contact: Elaine Shelton
E-Mail: ElaineShelton@worldnet.att.net
Website: http://www.sonic.net/thom/oor

Senior Beacon
P.O. Box 2227
Silver Spring, MD 20915-2227
Tel: (301) 608-0700; Fax: (301) 608-2145
E-mail: info@seniorbeacon.com
Website: http://www.seniornews.com/senior-beacon

Appendix G

Websites

AARP Network
http://www.aarp.org

ADD Warehouse, Resources for Attention Deficit Disorder and Related Problems
http://www.addwarehouse.com

American Cancer Society
http://www.cancer.org

Big Brothers/Big Sisters of America
http://www.bbbsa.org

Child Welfare League of America
http://www.cwla.org

DHHS Area Administration on Aging
http://www.aoa.dhhs.gov

Early Head Start National Resource Center (Zero to Three)
http://www.zerotothree.org

Family.com
http://www.family.com

Family Law Advisor (has page on grandparent issues)
http://www.divorcenet.com

Foundation for Grandparenting
http://www.grandparenting.org

Generations United
http://www.gu.org

Grand Parent Again
http://www.grandparentagain.com
E-mail address: saltybug@aol.com

Grandsplace: For Grandparents and Special Others Raising Children
http://www.grandsplace.com

Head Start Bureau Homepage
http://www.acf.dhhs.gov/programs/hsb/index.htm

Information Center and Link Site for Grandparents
http://www.geocities.com/heartland/hills/3157/grand.html

National Child Care Information Center
http://www.nccic.org

National Parent Information Network
http://www.npin.org

National Youth Gang Center
http://www.iir.com/nygc

New York State Citizens' Coalition for Children
http://www.nysccc.org

Parents Helping Parents (PHP, Inc.)
http://www.php.com

Parenthoodweb
http://www.parenthoodweb.com

Parentsoup
http://www.parentsoup.com

Parentsplace
http://www.parentsplace.com

Parents of Adult Children Addicts
http://www.geocities.com/heartland/estates/5081
Contact: Janelle Osborn
E-mail address: tarie2@home.com

Rocking Chair Gazette
http://www.wyndsong.com

Seniors Site
http://www.seniors-site.com

Third Age
http://www.thirdage.com

YMCA
http://www.ymca.net

Appendix H

International Resources

Australia/New Zealand

Aged Care Info Line
Tel: 1-800-500-853 (Australia)

Commonwealth Dept. of Health and Family Services
Central Office
GPO Box 9848
Canberra City, ACT 2601
Website: http://www.health.gov.au
Website has links to other services, including drug treatment,
disabilities, aged care, and international resources.

Crisis Care
Tel: (08) 9325-1111, 1-800-199-008 (Australia)

Department of Social Welfare
Private Bag 21
Wellington, 6001, New Zealand
Write for service information c/o Librarian.

Family and Children's Services
Central Office
189 Royal Street
East Perth, WA, 6004
        - or -
P.O. Box 6334
East Perth, WA, 6892
Tel: (08) 9222-2555; Fax: (08) 9222-2776, 1-800-622-258
Website: http://www.fcs.wa.gov.au
Has over 60 offices in Western Australia.

Family Helpline
Tel: (08) 9221-2000, 1-800-643-000 (Australia)

Office of Seniors Interests
Mary Holman Center, 4th Floor
32 St. Georges Terrace
Perth, Western Australia 6000
Tel: (08) 9220-1111; Fax: (08) 9221-2247

Parenting Line
Tel: (08) 9272-1466, 1-800-654-432 (Australia)

Canada

Age and Opportunity
200-283 Portage Ave.
Winnepeg, MB R3B 2B5
Tel: (204) 956-6440; Fax: (204) 946-5667

Canadian Association of Retired Persons
27 Queen St. East, Suite 1304
Toronto, ON M5C 2M6
Website: http://www.fifty-plus.net

Canadian Grandparents' Rights Association
260-3631 No. 3 Road
Richmond, BC V6X 2B9
Tel: (604) 273-GRAN (4726)
Fax: (604) 273-1823
Contact: Nancy Woodridge, President and Founder

Canadian Grandparents' Rights Association
5512 4th St. NW, Box 64128
Calgary, AB T2K 6J1
Tel: (403) 284-3887; Fax: same
Contact: Florence Knight

Child & Family Canada
http://www.cfc-efc.ca

Compassionate Friends of Canada
685 Willam Ave.
Winnepeg, MB R3E OZ2
Tel: (204) 475-9527; Fax: (204) 475-6693

Grandparents Raising Grandchildren
137-15215 105th Ave.
Surrey, BC V3R 1R9
Tel: (604) 951-0295
Contact: Marilyn Stevens

G.R.A.N.D.
Grandparents Requesting Access and Dignity
1516 Bourcier Dr.
Orleans, ON K1E 3J5
Tel: (613) 837-8371; Fax: same
Conatact: Lilliane George, President

Grandparents Rights Association Yukon
Box 165
Car Cross, YT Y0B 1B0
Tel: (867) 821-3821, (867) 863-5576, (867) 863-5812 (evenings)
Contact: Eleanor Millard

Growth Society
1998 Anthony Ave.
Ottawa, ON K2B 6T9
Tel: (613) 722-3310; Fax: (613) 722-6406
Contact: Madeleine Bremner

Info-Seniors: Canada's Guide to Senior Citizens' Resources
http://www.infoseniors.com

Office for Seniors
First Floor, 1515 Blanchard St.
Victoria, BC V8W 3C8
Tel: (250) 952-1238; Fax: (250) 952-1159

Order Form

Please Send Me:

_____ copies of *To Grandma's House, We...Stay*
@ $12.95 per copy   _____

California residents add 8.25% tax   _____

Postage & handling for one copy   ____$2.50____

Postage & handling for additional
copies @ 75¢ each   _____

TOTAL ENCLOSED   ══════════════

Payment Type

❏ Check   ❏ Money Order   ❏ Visa

❏ Mastercard   ❏ Discover   ❏ American Express

Credit Card #:_____ Exp. Date:_____

Name:_____

Address:_____

City:_____ State:_____ Zip:_____

Make checks payable to: ***Studio 4 Productions***
                                      P.O. Box 280400
                                  Northridge, CA 91328-0400
                                          U.S.A.